true love
PROJECT

true love PROJECT

how the GOSPEL defines your purity

clayton & sharie king

B&H
PUBLISHING GROUP
Nashville, Tennessee

978-1-4336-8433-3

Published by B&H Publishing Group
Nashville, Tennessee

Dewey Decimal Classification: 248.83
Subject Heading: CHRISTIAN LIFE \ LOVE \
INTIMACY (PSYCHOLOGY)

2 3 4 5 6 7 • 19 18 17 16 15

This book is dedicated to Joe and Jane King, my parents who adopted me when I was just a few weeks old. They didn't have a perfect marriage, but they stayed faithful to Christ and to each other all the way until death. They taught me more about love through their example than I could learn from a thousand books.—Clayton

Contents

"HOT NOW" vs. "Not Now"

Is anything better in this life than a Krispy Kreme doughnut?

The absolute best are the ones straight from the Krispy Kreme store, fresh out of the oven, warm and gooey, before the glaze even starts to crackle.

And did you know that most Krispy Kreme stores turn on a red sign in their front window when a fresh batch of doughnuts has just come out of the oven? It says, "HOT NOW." When you see that sign, get in there as quickly as possible. Waiting just beyond that red neon is an explosion of tasteful bliss that'll cost you less than a latte at Starbucks.

If you've ever had a Krispy Kreme doughnut, your brain is now reminding you of how good it tasted and how warm it felt in your mouth. If you've seen the "HOT NOW" sign before, that glowing red image flashed in your mind. And at this moment you're considering throwing this book down and running into town to grab a box (and a half gallon of milk).

You're welcome.

Of course, it sounds innocent enough when I'm talking about doughnuts, but the scary thing I've learned is that this is the same way many young people think about sex. It's appealing; it beckons. It's tempting because you know it's good (or at least you've been told it is), but you also know it can hurt you. It doesn't cost you anything because, if both people want to, it's free. And you can see "HOT NOW" signs everywhere you look. On Facebook. On billboards. On TV. If you're burning with desire, you can have sex now. A hookup. A booty call. A few clicks on the screen or taps on the phone, and you're in business.

Our culture has devalued sex to the point that it's considered with the flippancy of buying a box of doughnuts. It's no more serious to most people than an impulsive turn into a doughnut shop. As much thought goes into sex as it does into the flavor of doughnut you want. And honestly, most people take more time to consider the negative effects of buying a dozen doughnuts than they do sleeping together, experimenting sexually, or looking at porn.

Why Not?

So what's so bad about it?

Why should I abstain when everyone else is doing it?

If I'm smart enough to use protection, what's the big deal?

If both of us agree, what's wrong with it?

It's my body. Who are you to tell me what I can do with it?

These are all valid questions. I've asked every one of them myself. And together we will explore answers to every one of them. But the main reason we should get serious about sex and what we do with our bodies boils down to one thing. Paul explains, "Don't you know that your body is a sanctuary of the Holy Spirit who is in you, whom you have from God? You are not your own, for you were bought at a price. Therefore glorify God in your body" (1 Corinthians 6:19–20).

To his friends in Corinth, Paul points out the single most essential truth regarding sex. He wants them to understand that even though their entire culture was enjoying free and frequent sexual experiences, they were Christians, and they were different—they had been purchased by Jesus on the cross. Jesus paid a high price to liberate them from the slavery, guilt, and bondage of sexual sin. He gave His life for their freedom, and He gave them new purity, new holiness, and new identities.

The Backstory on Corinth

You understand that what God is asking of you seems impossible. If you're even considering following His standard for love and dating and sex, it means you're choosing to swim upstream against a tsunami of cultural pressure and expectations. It means you are defying the odds. You have the audacity to go against the tide. You may be singled out, and you will wonder if you're missing out on all the fun of experimenting with your sexual curiosities. You may feel like you're all alone.

But you're not alone.

Moreover, you're not even living in the most sex-obsessed culture that's ever existed. Things have been worse before. Way worse.

Almost two thousand years ago, a small group of Christians lived in the city of Corinth. These are the same people Paul was speaking to in the verses above about their battle for sexual purity and holiness. Much as I'm writing these pages to help you, he wrote page after page to his Corinthian friends to help them. He encouraged them. He instructed them. He corrected them. He even rebuked them. Because he loved them and wanted the best for them, he admonished them to live lives that were set apart for the mission Jesus had given them to be witnesses of His gospel.

Corinth sat on the ocean, so it became a strategic port city for ships to dock. These ships would come from all over the world bringing goods to trade like gold and salt and silk and spices. Visitors and sailors were constantly coming into the city on ships and by road to bring goods to trade.

Along with the trade industry, another major business developed: prostitution. The ancient Greek and Roman worlds viewed sex as a commodity. People felt no shame in public displays of sexuality. Censorship did not exist. Sexual self-control was unheard of. Sexual appetites were meant to be fulfilled, and sexuality was celebrated and flaunted. So as Corinth became a major economic hub that attracted men from all over the world, those men often expected to have lots of sex when they arrived in Corinth.

The men got sex. The pimps who ran the industry got rich. And the prostitutes got used.

When I visited the remains of the city in 2004, the museum there contained artifacts and pottery and statues that testified to the prominence of the sex industry. Without going into too much detail, let's just say that they were so obsessed with sex that the cups they drank out of and the plates they ate off of celebrated sexual encounters.

That was two thousand years ago. Their culture was depraved and confused just like ours. They were sinners just like us. And Christians had to swim upstream just like you. God didn't change His standards or expectations for them just because it was hard. He won't change them for your generation either.

God loves you and wants the best for you. He will continue to call you to holiness and purity. He will always be leading us and empowering us to live lives that are set apart for Him and His mission of redeeming and restoring the world.

You're a child of God, dearly beloved, and on a mission in a culture that's lost and confused. You're part of God's rescue mission to bring people into His kingdom. You represent the gospel in everything you do and say, especially in how you conduct your relationships and handle your body. The way you treat the opposite sex, the ways you entertain yourself, the images you view, the temptations you flee, and the sexual standards you live by are all ways you testify that you belong to Jesus Christ.

Not Now

Throughout this whole cultural sex war, we tend to forget one thing: God didn't say sex was bad—quite the opposite. He created woman so that man would not be alone and commanded them to multiply! God made sex, and sex is good.

But God did say sex should happen within certain healthy guidelines. Outside of those guidelines we can expect consequences. So God isn't saying no; He's saying "not now." As a young, unmarried person, although you may have both the desire and the availability for sex, God's Word offers a healthier approach than "HOT NOW."

Hence the *True Love Project*.

Within the pages of this book, we'll talk about those guidelines and the consequences for not following them. We'll see the scientific evidence that backs up God's Word and discuss the *real* reasons for staying pure. I'll show you the power you've been given to make it happen and offer hope to those who feel they've already ruined their chances. Above all that, we'll discover that the ultimate goal has little to do with sex and everything to do with Jesus.

Project: Impossible

My mother was fifteen and unmarried when she had me. I was practically born knowing the struggles with sexual sin. I know that this mission for purity, this *True Love Project*, is impossible to do alone.

But we are not alone.

We have the Creator of the universe—an all-powerful, all-knowing God—on our side, fighting for us, encouraging us to hold on, to fight.

Our lives matter, and so does what we do with our bodies. If you are just beginning to understand and explore your sexuality, this is for you. If you feel dirty and condemned because you didn't wait, this study is for you too. This project is for all of us, to strengthen our lives and to help us come together in a closer walk with God, to guide us in glorifying Him with all we do.

I pray that wherever you are in your journey, this book will help to light your path. I hope you will find a solid basis for maintaining your purity and that it will be anchored in Christ—our only pure example of true love.

CHAPTER 1

God's Story, Your Story

"For I know the plans I have for you"—this is the Lord's declaration—"plans for your welfare, not for disaster, to give you a future and a hope."
—Jeremiah 29:11

Few people can resist a good story.

A riveting book, a blockbuster movie, or a friend at school telling what happened last weekend—there's something about a great story that draws you in and keeps you there. Sure, some people prefer adventure; others prefer a good mystery. I enjoy historical documentaries, and my wife enjoys adventure and drama. But whether you'd rather watch a romantic comedy or read a fantasy novel, the magnetic pull is the same. To be a good story, it must first contain some basic, essential elements.

The Plot

This is the big idea that everything revolves around, and you can usually tell what it is pretty early. A guy is trying to win the love of a lady. Two people who were separated are desperately trying to be reunited. A detective is solving a crime. Mystical creatures are on an epic quest to throw a powerful ring into the fires of Mount Doom. The Nazis are trying to capture the ark of the covenant (my personal favorite, *Raiders of the Lost Ark*). Or a werewolf and a vampire are fighting over the same girl (not that I know anything about that . . . a friend told me).

The Characters

These are the people who move the plot along. The more involved the characters are with the plot, the more invested you become in the story. Often you can tell who the good guys are and who the bad guys are. Other stories leave more ambiguity with traces of both good and bad in the main characters. You can also call them the protagonist (good guy, main character) and the antagonist (bad guy, the enemy). You could even boil it down to the hero and the villain. Then the other supporting characters come alongside the hero and villain and play specific roles in the overall plot. As the story moves along, the characters develop, and we begin to learn about them: their backstories, their strengths, their flaws, and their fears. We connect with these characters as they play their roles in the bigger story.

The Conflict

Without conflict there is no story. That's what makes a movie worth paying money to see. Early on in any good book, you recognize a major problem that threatens to thwart the plot. Without this element, the author has no story to tell. You see a problem emerge that needs to be solved. Although the characters may help connect us to the story, the drama keeps us involved and interested. As soon as the main character becomes involved in the plot, things become difficult. The plot has resistance. Overcoming that resistance (solving the problem) demands our attention. Whether it's a dragon to be slain, an outlaw to be brought to justice, or a relationship to be fixed, the drama that emerges from the crisis is what causes us to invest emotionally in the story.

The Resolution

Ah, the happy ending. The plot has unfolded as the main character has fought through adversity and crisis, villains and bad guys, and the problem is eventually solved. The guy and the girl wind up in each other's arms. The nuclear warhead was disarmed as the countdown clock hit 0:02. The clues finally came together, and the criminal was caught moments before she struck her next victim. Through tenacity, perseverance, and some good luck, the problem was resolved, the hero comes out on top, and things turn out for the best. The resolution makes everyone feel happy.

As I said, everyone loves a good story. But why is that? What about us, deep inside of us, keeps us coming back, even when we've read dozens of books and seen hundreds of hours of drama and romance and adventure on the big screen? Is there something intrinsic about *story* that we find appealing? Does something inside of us have a soul-hunger for the story?

And ultimately, what does all of this have to do with love and relationships?

God's Story

The reason we connect so quickly and so deeply with smaller stories is because we are all part of a much bigger, more important story that has been playing out since the dawn of human history.

It's a story written by God Himself. He is the main character, and His Son, Jesus, is the hero. We are part of the cast of characters, and the plot revolves around a pretty big problem: a cosmic mutiny, a universal resistance to God and His ways.

We have all rebelled against God. We have turned our backs on Him and been deceived into believing we don't need Him. We've committed treason against His loving rule over our world and have decided to do things our way, regardless of His commands. The villain goes by several names: Satan, Lucifer, the devil, the accuser, the evil one. He hates God, and he hates us because we were made in God's image. His ultimate desire is to steal from us, kill us, and destroy us. But God is working His big idea to save us and rescue us from destruction.

> A thief comes only to steal and to kill and to destroy. I have come so that they may have life and have it in abundance. (John 10:10)

We need to be saved from impending doom. We must be redeemed from our sin and the consequences of our rebellion. We must be rescued from our selfishness and our desire to live only for pleasure and not for God and one another. We must be liberated from Satan who plans and plots our demise every moment of every day.

Before any of us were drawn into the smaller stories we love in movies and books and TV shows, we were already part of an ancient, larger story. The story we find ourselves in is older than we are. It is bigger than we are. It is of greater eternal importance than we could ever fathom. Because you were made by God in His own image, you carry His image throughout your life. You reflect God's creativity, and you bear His resemblance. You are a part of His bigger, eternal story that began when He created the first humans in His image and to have stewardship over all the earth.

You may have never thought about what it means to be made in God's image, or that you are blessed by God just because you are a human, or that God has work for you to do in this world. But these verses from the first chapter of Genesis introduce us to God's story and *your* role in it. First and foremost, our identity—your identity—is that of the image bearers of God.

We can learn a few things from

> Then God said, "Let Us make man in Our image, according to Our likeness. They will rule the fish of the sea, the birds of the sky, the livestock, all the earth, and the creatures that crawl on the earth." So God created man in His own image; He created him in the image of God; He created them male and female. God blessed them, and God said to them, "Be fruitful, multiply, fill the earth, and subdue it." (Genesis 1:26–28)

the opening act, the first chapter, or the introduction to the story.

- God made us because He wanted to. No one forced Him to create you. He designed you with purpose and skill.
- You were fashioned and designed in God's image. You are His image bearer.
- God established order with the first human proto- types. He made a man and a woman to live together, work together, fit together, and reflect the "Us" of God, meaning the Trinity of Father, Son, and Holy Spirit.
- From the beginning, God ordained and commanded men and women to have sex, both as a sign of the covenant and promise of marriage and as the physical means of multiplying the human race. He specifies sex as a gift given to a man and a woman, exclusively and with value and purpose.
- Men and women are given authority by God to sub- due all of His creation, exercising stewardship as His managers and obeying His gracious and loving order of creation.

Every good story reflects God's story, and His story (which is our story, as well) has four essential parts.

1. Creation

The biblical witness of history tells us God created all things out of nothing. He was preexistent to our world, our solar system, and our universe. Out of His own wisdom and power, He chose to create—water and land, day and night, fish and birds, animals and insects, and eventually the crown jewel of creation: people. He thought us up. Then He made us. Like an engineer who designs a car engine from scratch, no one is better equipped to explain or repair that engine than the engineer who designed it. If anyone knows what is best for us, God does. He created humanity for His own glory and for relationships with one another and with Him.

His initial design for the human race at creation was for us to live and love and to work. God created an entire planet with an ecosystem to sustain life for us. He provided animals and water and seeds and plants. He endowed us with authority to rule over His world as stewards. He wisely created one species of human life with two genders that could procreate and populate the earth with more humans who could live and love and work and enjoy God and His good gifts. He knew that in spite of Adam's having a relationship with God, he needed another level of intimacy. So God provided him with a woman, a wife, a partner, a helper who was part of his own flesh.

From the beginning of human life, God revealed His intent in the order of creation. It was not random or circumstantial.

God did things on purpose. He was deliberate in His design. Creating male and female provided each with more than just the physical anatomy to create more life. It provided them, and us, with the source of love and affection and support and friendship we all need—another person that is like us as a human, yet different from us in gender.

This was God's idea and His design for men and women. Attraction is not a sin. On the contrary we are hardwired to notice the opposite sex, to sense a longing and need for them, and ultimately to enter into a covenant relationship with them called marriage. Although some have a special gift to remain single, most of us will follow God's plan that He implemented at the dawn of human life with Adam and Eve, and we will make a promise to a mate to love that one person faithfully in this life, no matter what comes our way. And every time a couple marries, they reflect the wisdom and glory God unveiled in Eden when He ordained the first marriage relationship.

First and foremost our identity is that of the image bearers of God. We were not originally wicked, sinful, worthless, hopeless, doomed, and condemned. We became that way through rebellion against God. His original blueprint was that we look like Him, reflecting His own relationship within the Trinity (Father, Son, Spirit) as we love one another in friendships and marriage. Returning to this primary, original design is the ultimate end of God's story.

2. The Fall

In the midst of the perfect environment of God's creation, filled with life and wonder and work and pleasure, God
graciously allowed Adam and Eve to enjoy all the good gifts
that grew in the garden. However, God forbade them to have
one item. It was a fruit tree that was named "the tree of the
knowledge of good and evil." God lovingly warned the couple
to avoid that tree. God knew that tree had the potential to
affect them eternally if they ate from its branches. To protect
them He warned, "But you must not eat from the tree of the
knowledge of good and evil, for on the day you eat from it,
you will certainly die" (Genesis 2:17).

Now don't get so caught up in the specifics that you miss
the obvious. The Bible doesn't give us all the details about the
tree or what the fruit looked like or how it tasted. God knew
some things we don't know, and even Adam and Eve didn't
know. The obvious implication is that God reserved that tree
as off-limits. He graciously gave them enough information to
spare them from death, and He had already provided them
with all they could ever need or want. He gave them food.
He gave them a companion. He gave them dominion. He gave
them instructions. He gave them personal interaction with
Him in a loving, intimate relationship.

And He also gave them a choice. They were able to decide
if they trusted God's heart for them. Did they believe He had
only good intentions for them, or did they secretly wonder if He

was being unfair by fencing off one small piece of their garden and claiming it as His own? Did they wonder if God was holding out on them, keeping something good and powerful from them that would make them happier than they already were?

We don't know at what point they began to doubt or question God's intentions, but we do know they acted in rebellion and disobedience. The Bible tells us that a serpent came into the garden and questioned God's intent in prohibiting them from eating from the forbidden tree. "Now the serpent was the most cunning of all the wild animals that the LORD God had made. He said to the woman, 'Did God really say, "You can't eat from any tree in the garden"?' . . . 'No! You will not die,' the serpent said to the woman. 'In fact, God knows that when you eat it your eyes will be opened and you will be like God, knowing good and evil'" (Genesis 3:1, 4–5).

In other words the serpent told them, "God is keeping something from you that you would love and enjoy. He doesn't really love you. If He did, He wouldn't withhold this from you. He is afraid that if you eat this fruit, your eyes would be opened. You would grow stronger. He would feel threatened by you. He is afraid to lose control. Don't let Him manipulate you. Nothing is off-limits! No one has the right to tell you what you can and cannot do. Go ahead and take it."

This is where the story takes a dramatic turn. Adam and Even were deceived, and they disobeyed. They rebelled against the God who made them and gave them all good things. They took the fruit and ate it, believing they could be like God, knowing all things. Immediately their eyes were opened but not to greater pleasure and more happiness. The serpent had lied. They saw their shame, their nakedness, and their sin. They tried to hide from God, embarrassed at their mutiny against God's gracious goodness.

We call this "the fall." After they sinned, they were never the same, and neither are we. Every human since that day has been born with a fallen nature into a fallen, broken world where each of us rebels against God and chooses to believe lies instead of His truth. We see in Adam and Eve a reflection of our own selves. We doubt God's intent. We don't trust His goodness. We think we know better than God. We believe He is withholding something from us that would make us happier. We forget His warnings and foolishly plow ahead into forbidden territory.

And like our most ancient ancestors, we pay a heavy price for it.

3. Redemption

The result of our rebellion and sin against God and His love is tragic. Romans 6:23 says, "The wages of sin is death." Simply put, our sin has a serious consequence.

The endgame is not, as the serpent said, greater knowledge and more power. It is eternal death and separation from

God. It's the ultimate bait and switch: our hearts deceive us into believing God and His order are irrelevant or unimportant, so we strike out on our own to do things our way. For a season we enjoy the pleasure of our rebellion and the momentary rush of doing something we wanted badly, but as soon as the thrill is gone, we're like Adam and Eve in the garden, realizing that we made a huge mistake, wondering if God can see us exposed, and trying to cover up our sin and sweep things under the rug.

Yet the damage has been done, and we ourselves can do absolutely nothing to reverse or undo what we have broken. The wages of our sin kick in. The consequences begin to unfold. Like a man who smoked cigarettes his whole life and then finds out at age fifty-five he's dying of lung cancer, sin silently works its destruction in our lives until eventually it destroys us.

The relationship between humanity and God was broken, and we desperately need to be reconciled. As John Calvin said, "For the holiest of men cannot hope to obtain anything from God until he has been freely reconciled to Him."

What we need is not self-help or modest improvements. Positive thinking can't make a dent in our real problem. We can't think our way out of the hole we dig for ourselves. We must be reconciled. We need to be saved.

We need someone to rescue us who is bigger, stronger, and smarter than we are.

This is exactly what God does for us, and He does it through His Son, Jesus Christ. This is the part of the story where the crisis is at its apex, and it feels like things can't possibly get better. Then, in an unlikely twist, God crashes into the middle of the problem, not in the form of a military general or an all-powerful Caesar or an unstoppable superhero, but in the form of a . . . *baby?*

Against all common sense and human expectation, God doesn't send a conqueror or a warrior to rescue His people. He sends a newborn baby, birthed in a no-name town to a no-name mother with no pedigree to make Him stand out. Through this little Baby born in a small Middle Eastern town, God intends to set things straight for all humanity. This divine act is known by many names: salvation, reconciliation, being born again, rescued, saved, becoming a Christian, trusting Christ, and finding life.

But the word that best describes this process of being rescued from sin and destruction is *redemption*. It's a word that embodies a rich and deep understanding of God's decisive and sacrificial act of winning us back from an enemy that had taken us captive. It helps us understand the scandalous nature of His decision to purchase us out of slavery to sin. It paints a beautiful picture of the divine exchange God initiated on our behalf, where He traded His Son for our pardon and gave His life in exchange for ours. Ultimately, it unveils the great mystery of God's sovereign decision to pay the penalty we owed for our sin and rebellion by taking our place on the cross. Not only that, but the perfect obedience of Jesus was credited to us so that we can stand before God with the righteousness of Christ.

Jesus lived the perfect life we could never live. He died the horrible death we deserved to die. He was raised from death to give us new life. He gives us His Spirit to lead us and change us. *This is redemption.*

Shadows of God's redemption are seen in the Old Testament story of Moses leading the Jewish slaves out of Egyptian bondage. They are set free, delivered, bought back, and rescued from the tyranny of a ruthless dictator. They pass through the waters of the Red Sea on their way to a place God had prepared for them called the promised land. This foreshadows what God does for us in Jesus.

As the Israelites were held captive in Egypt, we are held captive in sin.

As God sent Moses to redeem them, God sent Jesus to redeem us.

As the children of Israel passed through the waters of the Red Sea on their way to Canaan, we pass through the waters of baptism on our way to salvation and, ultimately, heaven.

As God had prepared a land for the Jews to inhabit, Jesus has promised us a place in His Father's house and a place at the table at the marriage feast of the Lamb. We are rescued. We are liberated. We are reconciled. We are redeemed.

4. Restoration

God's intent is not just to spare you from hell. He wants more than a few million individual Christians that make it through the pearly gates. God has a much bigger plan for all of His creation. He never gave up on the world He started in Eden. To be sure, He has been working since that day Adam and Eve turned their back on Him to break the curse of sin and make all things new by establishing His kingdom on Earth through His people.

He doesn't just want to save us. He wants to restore us to the place He originally intended us to be—with Him in loving fellowship, living together in a world created to sustain life and joy.

God will restore our broken relationship with Him when we repent of sin and trust Christ alone for salvation.

God will restore creation to a place filled with life and joy and work and wonder and worship. It will look something like Eden, though I can't really talk specifics because it's a fool's game to try to predict what God has envisioned.

And God will restore our relationships with one another, how we talk to and treat one another, how we forgive and support one another. We will once and for all know how to give and receive love.

But I want you to think of restoration not just as something that happens one day out in the future. I want you to see restoration right here, right now, available to you immediately and permanently. You don't have to wait until Jesus returns to experience this. He is already doing a work of restoration in you if you belong to Him.

That restoration touches every part of your life, but it particularly repairs and renews your perspective on love and relationships. Remember that God began creation with a man and a woman. He made them to belong to each other, one flesh, and gave them the ability to love and care for each other and for children they would make together. The fall altered God's perfect design, but Jesus makes restoration possible. That restoration isn't waiting until the return of Jesus to get started. It is already in effect in you right now!

It affects the way you relate to the opposite sex. It changes how you see your sexuality, your desires, your own body, and your craving for affection and attention. It transforms your expectations from your boyfriend or girlfriend. It calls you to serve and sacrifice for the person you love as the culture around you continues to use and manipulate people for pleasure. Restoration means you don't let sexual cravings, emotional loneliness, or past mistakes control you. Instead, you are controlled by the Holy Spirit, who is living and working in you.

That is what the *True Love Project* is all about.

I want to help you understand God's eternal, bigger story. I want you to see the big picture from the beginning in Eden until right now. I want you to see your part in the story—where you fit in, why you matter, and what God wants to do with you and through you.

This story is bigger than you alone. It's about way more than falling in love and waiting until you're married to have sex. Jesus is the hero of the story. He saves the day. So whether you get married or remain single for life, Jesus is the treasure. Whether you're a virgin until your wedding day or struggle to believe you're forgiven by Christ for your sexual sins, Jesus is the treasure. He is the perfect example of true love.

You will be more satisfied if you do relationships the way God originally intended. You can avoid the regret, the shame, the guilt, and the depression. You can be forgiven for the sins and the mistakes of your past. You can be a witness to the fact that Jesus has redeemed your life, realigned your allegiances, reorganized your expectations, restored your broken soul, and renewed your hope for true love.

You don't have to stumble blindly through life wondering if God knows your situation or if God has a plan and a will for your life. His story unfolds in Scripture, and He graciously gives you guidance in its pages. The Bible clearly communicates His expectations and leaves little open for debate when it says, "For this is God's will, your sanctification: that you abstain from sexual immorality, so that each of you knows how to control his own body in sanctification and honor, not with lustful desires, like the Gentiles who don't know God" (1 Thessalonians 4:3–5).

You can have true love, but not until you have embraced the love that will last through the ages, given to you freely by Jesus Christ as His beloved daughters and sons. With Jesus as your example, the Holy Spirit as your teacher, and the Scriptures as your guide, you can honor God and serve others in your relationships. You can be prepared for the person God is preparing to be your mate. And the two of you can serve Christ together as witnesses of His power to redeem and restore.

The goal is not just to be a virgin on your wedding day. It's much bigger than that. The goal is to be found faithful on judgment day. That's a vision worth living for. That is a story worth joining.

> Sex simply cannot fill the cosmic need for closure that our souls seek in romance. Only meeting Christ face to face will fill the emptiness in our hearts that sin created when we lost our unbroken fellowship with him.
> Timothy Keller, *The Meaning of Marriage*[1]

True Talk

1. What do God, Adam, and Eve have to do with your story that's unfolding *right now?*

2. What if Adam and Eve had ignored the serpent and stayed away from the fruit? Would you be reading this book, answering this question right now? Explain.

3. How would you describe the elements of your own story?
Plot:
Characters:
Conflict:
Resolution:

CHAPTER 2

The Cost of Ownership

Choose for yourselves this day who you will serve.
—Joshua 24:15 (NIV)

Before you can understand love, you must understand lordship. Before you decide whom you will love, you must decide who is your lord.

Every single important thing in your life revolves around this one issue. All the major decisions you will ever make can be traced back to this question. The way you treat others, the expectations you carry into relationships, the limits you impose upon yourself sexually—these will all reflect the answer to the most essential question in all of life.

Who Is Your Lord?

The word *lord* carries weight and authority. In more current language we'd think of words like *master, boss, ruler,* and *king.* Someone who calls the shots. The person you answer to, the person whose opinion you consider before making decisions—that person is the lord of your life.

And that person can be anyone, really. It can be you, your parents, a friend, a teacher, or even the president. It can even be attainable things, like money or popularity.

But might I suggest that the one who is most qualified to be your lord isn't any tangible thing or even a mere human being? He is the one and only Lord Jesus Christ. This Lord is more powerful than the president, more influential than a prime minister, more prominent than a king or a queen, with more authority than a government or the United Nations. Now imagine this authority not on a planetary scale that only involves Earth but on a universal scale that includes all other planets, solar systems, universes, and the entirety of the vast cosmos. Only then will you get a tiny glimpse into the concept of lordship as it applies to Jesus.

Jesus Christ rules and reigns over every square inch of the entire universe. He declares that all of it belongs to Him, and He is well within His rights to make this claim because He *created* everything He claims as His own. Jesus is Lord of all things—the things we can see and everything else we can't see or have never observed.

This, my friends, is lordship on a grand, universal scale.

But what about lordship on a personal level? And what does it have to do with sex, relationships, dating, and what you do with your body?

It has *everything* to do with it. I'll go a step further. Not only is this important to your views and beliefs about love and intimacy and marriage, but lordship is the most crucial and essential issue you will deal with *in the entirety of your life*. It's more important than who you date, where you attend college, what job you take, where you live, how many kids you have, or how much money you make. The question of lordship is the foundation for every choice and decision you make about everything that will ever matter in your life. I couldn't possibly exaggerate or overstate this simple truth:

> *Whoever has the title "lord" in your life is the decisive ruler of your life.*

And, ultimately, it boils down to two choices: it's either Jesus or it's you.

When Jesus is Lord . . .

You realize how much He loves you and cares for you. You recognize the sacrifice He made to save you when He died in your place to remove your sin and reconcile you to God. You are amazed at the grace He gave you and the mercy He shows you every day. You gladly submit your whole life to Him because you believe He is wiser and smarter than you are. You desire for Him to guide and rule your life because you trust that He wants what's best for you.

When Jesus is Lord, you want to honor His Word in your relationships and live by His rules that govern your body and your desires. When He is Lord, you submit sexual appetites and affections to His law, you heed His warnings, and you practice obedience to His commands. In return He protects you from the consequences of sexual sin, and He provides you with the grace to live day by day in repentance, submission, and forgiveness in a community of sisters and brothers who will help you on your journey.

When you are lord . . .

You're driven primarily by whatever you want at any given moment—food or drugs, sex or success, money or materialism. If you are the lord of your life, then you are the ultimate authority, and you become a god unto yourself.

You may have never thought of it in those terms, but that's exactly how most people live their lives. The only thing they consider before making a decision is whether it will give them pleasure. You don't care if it hurts someone else in the short run or if it hurts you in the long run. You don't stop to think if it is the right thing to do or the wise thing to do or if there will be consequences years down the road. The only thought is right here, right now, getting what you want. When you are lord of your own life, nobody can ever tell you to stop. No one can say, *"No, don't do that!"* because you are the only one with authority to make that call. You gave yourself that authority, and you won't let anyone take it from you. Not even Jesus. So if you're accustomed to doing what you want or doing what others tell you will make you happy, you will also act that way when it comes to love and dating and sex.

True Story

I was speaking at a public school assembly and talking about sex. I was being very honest with the students about how powerful sex is: how it can become addictive and how it can hurt and devastate teenagers.

After the assembly a sixteen-year-old girl approached me, and she was upset.

"Who do you think you are? You can't tell me who I can sleep with or what I can do with my boyfriend, or my girl-friend, or even a perfect stranger I meet at a party. It's my body, and I will do what I want to with it!"

That is the attitude of someone who has decided that she is her own lord.

And unfortunately she was right.

When she assumed that position of ultimate authority, she took on the responsibility of making all her own choices based on what she wanted. What she didn't realize, however, is that each of those choices—"hooking up" with strangers at parties and all the sexual curiosity she explored with her partners—has consequences.

God will allow you to be your own lord if that is what you want. But when it comes time to pay the price, you will be the one to pay it.

Why would we ever choose that path when Jesus openly offers a much better plan? He's already paid the price for our sins if we only choose to make Him Lord. We allow ourselves to get so wrapped up in our egos that we argue no one has the right to tell us what to do. We know what's best for ourselves, thankyouverymuch.

But the truth is, simply put: we are just too small to be Lord.

Too Small to Be Lord

The job of ultimate ruler, boss, and master needs to be filled by someone who has what it takes to call the shots. It needs to be someone who can handle the job, who is smart and experienced enough to see things you don't see and to know things you couldn't possibly know. It needs to be someone with a firm grasp on the facts as well as the future, someone who can look down the road and know how to steer your life clear from destruction and devastation. Do you really think you are that person?

The only person qualified to be Lord is Jesus Christ. He created the world. He created you. That takes wisdom and understanding. He gave His life to rescue you and me from sin and death. That takes compassion. He rose from the dead. That takes power. Is anyone more qualified to be Lord than Jesus? I don't think so.

My wife's uncle was a chief speechwriter for a former United States president. He showed us pictures of him and the president together in the Oval Office. He told us stories about the things the president had to deal with on a daily basis. As he described the decisions the president had to make and all the factors he had to consider and all the voices he had to listen to, I felt my stomach begin to churn. Just the thought of being under that kind of pressure made me feel sick. I could never imagine being in a position with that much authority and that much responsibility.

It takes a special person to be the president. I'm not cut out for it. I couldn't juggle all the pressures, factor in all the details, filter through all the facts, consider all the perspectives, and make definite decisions that affect the United States and the whole world.

In the same way none of us is cut out to be Lord. We don't have what it takes to manage our own lives, not to mention the entire universe. But Jesus has what it takes; He's the only one who does.

The issue is not who is smarter or bigger or stronger or more powerful. You already know that it is Jesus, hands down. No, the issue isn't who is more qualified to be the Lord of your life.

The issue is whether or not you're willing to give up control to Him.

Do you trust Jesus with your relationships? Are you willing to trust Him with your sexual desires? Would you even be willing to trust Him with your past, your mistakes, and your regrets? When you decide you don't want to be lord anymore and you declare that Jesus is Lord, then by definition that means He calls the shots. *All the shots.* That includes who you hang out with. That includes what you watch on the Internet and what you look at on your phone. That includes who you date. And that includes what you do with the person you date.

Jesus looks at every square inch of the world and claims it as His own. He also sees every square inch of your life, your past and your future, and says, "Mine." If anyone else dared to make that claim, you'd think he was a dictator, a madman, or a control freak because we know that if another person tries to control us, he or she only wants to use us for selfish purposes.

So why would you ever allow Jesus to rule over you and control your life, your relationships, your desires?

Because He *is* true love.

Jesus is not selfish. He has no self-seeking desires. He has no insecurities. Jesus is God in the flesh, and He is completely perfect. He's never sinned. He's never had a bad thought. He would never take advantage of you or use you to make Himself feel better. Because He is God, He doesn't need anything; He is self-sufficient. That means He would never use you to get something for Himself. If He wanted or needed something, He could just take it. You see, that's what it means to be God; He is already perfect and never needs anything of any sort. At all. Ever. So if Jesus never needs anything, He would never try to use you to get something for Himself. He's not on a power trip. He's not a control freak.

So, why then does He want to be Lord so badly? If He doesn't need anything, what motivates Him to want to be in control of your life?

One word: *LOVE*.

Jesus loves you. His love is unlike any love you've ever known. It's perfect. Unconditional. No strings attached. He loves you for your sake. He wants what is best for you. He wants to protect you from harm. He wants to rescue you from sin. He wants to deliver you from temptation. He wants to shield you from pain.

He cares about you, and He knows best. He can see the consequences of your sins and bad decisions. And He invites you to give control of your life to Him, following His commands and living by His Word, because He knows that if you do things His way, you will be happier, you will experience a fuller life, and you will, in turn, be a witness to others about His love.

So when Jesus claims to be Lord, it's not arrogant or proud. It's loving. It's compassionate. It's true. He really is Lord, God, Master, Boss, Ruler, and King. The best thing He can do for us is to claim rightful ownership over us. The worst thing He could do for us would be to sit by and watch us try to act as if we were really lord. How cruel would it be for God to sit on the sidelines and allow us to destroy our relationships and our bodies with sexual sin and selfish indulgences and never warn us to repent!

We Protect What We Value

One Saturday afternoon my oldest son Jacob and I were picking up sticks in our front yard after a storm when one of our neighbors pulled in the driveway on his motorcycle. This was no normal bike. It was a brand-new Harley-Davidson with shiny chrome rims and handlebars, leather seats and saddlebags. He had paid more than $25,000 for the bike.

It was shiny and loud when he pulled up, but it was also hot. I'm talking really hot. I could feel the heat emanating from the engine. It was summertime, we were standing on asphalt, and he had been riding the bike for several hours, so it was hot.

Did I mention it was really, really hot?

My son Jacob had been drawn to machines since he could crawl. He loved tractors and trucks and bulldozers and lawn mowers. If it made noise, he wanted to ride it. He also loved things that sparkled, like shiny chrome exhaust pipes on Harley-Davidson motorcycles.

You know where this is going.

As I was talking to my neighbor, my three-year-old son inched closer and closer to the bike. Neither one of us noticed until both of his tiny hands reached for the chrome-plated exhaust pipe. I could already see the blisters, feel the burn, hear the cries. At that moment the love I had for my son instinctively forced me into action. I yelled in my sternest father voice, "NO, NO, NO, NOO!!!" I jumped between him and the bike and grabbed him with both hands, pulling him away a split second before his fingers met the singe of the exhaust pipes.

Because I value my son, I had to protect him.

He had no idea the kind of pain he would suffer from grabbing hold of that pipe. It was deceptively shiny and intriguing, inviting the curiosity of a three-year-old mind. But I knew. I know how motorcycles work; I've felt the sting of a burn.

And I'm his dad. I'm not only given the wisdom to know the things that will hurt my son; I'm also given the responsibility to stop him from hurting himself. *If I love him, I will warn him. I will protect him.* My booming voice may frighten, and my sudden grasp may startle, but I will do everything in my power to protect him, to place myself between him and danger in order to spare him from unnecessary pain.

And we get that, right?

But when it comes to God, a powerful Protector we cannot see, this concept tends to be more difficult to grasp. And yet what God does for us is on an exponentially larger scale. His love for us is boundless and unconditional, and that is His sole motivation. He's not on a power trip; He is omnipotent, all-powerful. He can't get any more powerful by bossing you around. He is motivated purely and intensely by love.

He exercises His authority in your life precisely because of His love for you. He wants to warn you, to protect you, to place Himself between you and harm. If I, as a mere human, instinctively know how to do that for my son, imagine how God desires to stop you from hurting yourself with sin.

This is why God has created boundaries for you. This is why He communicates His design for sex. He's not trying to keep you from having fun. He's trying to keep you from destroying yourself.

He understands how those relationships can become a beautiful blessing to you, as both friendships and eventually marriage—*He designed them that way.* Yet He also knows how much damage you can do when all you see is the shiny, attractive chrome, and your instincts tell you to grab it. You may not see the injury and regret beneath the shiny surface. But God does; He's your Father. And His responsibility is to do all He can to stop you from grabbing something that has the potential to hurt you deeply.

G. K. Chesterton effectively illustrated this idea of protecting what you value. He described a scene where little children were playing on the top of a beautiful mountain. However, a dangerous cliff lay just a few feet from where the children played. If they were to fall off the edge, they would certainly die. He asked the question: Is it more loving to allow them to play near the cliff freely with no boundaries, or is it more loving to place a fence between them and the edge? Are they freer to enjoy themselves with or without the fence?[1]

God establishes "sexual fences" to keep us from plunging into a deadly abyss. We are not "free" when we climb over those boundaries; we are falling. We are only truly free when we enjoy sex and love inside the protection and safety of God's design, when we trust God's intentions for us.

This is precisely why God expresses His design for sex, His intentions for love, and His delight in marriage. He wants us to enjoy His creation, to thrive in relationships with our sisters and brothers, and to experience the greatest intimacy as it was intended: becoming one flesh in marriage and sexual union with your mate.

God initiated this design from the beginning, and Jesus affirms that in His answer to the Pharisees' question about marriage:

> The Bible does not counsel sexual abstinence before marriage because it has such a low view of sex but because it has such a lofty one.—Timothy Keller, *The Meaning of Marriage*[2]

"'Haven't you read,' He replied, 'that He who created them in the beginning made them male and female,' and He also said: 'For this reason a man will leave his father and mother and be joined to his wife, and the two will become one flesh? So they are no longer two, but one flesh. Therefore, what God has joined together, man must not separate'" (Matthew 19:4–6).

What Jesus told the Pharisees then is still true today. God created you. God created man's need for a woman and woman's need for a man. And when you decide who is lord of your life, you also decide whether or not you choose to follow God's design.

So, who's in charge of your life? The answer to that question will determine the decisions you make, the kind of person you become, and your ultimate eternal destiny. Is it you? Or is it Jesus?

Jesus Is Jealous

Jealousy is a bad thing, right? I mean, nobody likes jealous friends. Who wants friends who always get mad because you spend more time with someone else than them? When we notice jealousy in a boyfriend or a girlfriend, we feel smothered and controlled because we just want them to trust us and not be so insecure.

So, is jealousy ever good? Yes, of course!

When I met my wife, we were in our twenties, and we had both dated other people. As a matter of fact, I had just ended a four-year relationship, and she had just broken off an engagement. This was a challenge for us both. She wondered if I still had feelings for my ex, and I wondered how big the diamond ring was that she gave back to her ex-fiancé.

I also wondered if I could take him in a fair fight. I was pretty sure I could.

Our love for each other generated jealousy. I didn't want her to talk to her ex-boyfriend. I didn't want her to think about him. I wanted her affection and her attention. Just the thought of the two of them together made my blood pressure rise.

Sharie was feeling the same thing about my ex-girlfriend. And it all culminated one night when my phone rang. I answered, and it was my ex. She had heard that I'd broken my collarbone in a motorcycle accident and was calling to see if I was OK. We hadn't spoken in more than a year, so I was surprised to hear from her. I was also surprised about thirty seconds after I had answered the phone when Sharie walked into the room and asked whom I was talking to. Imagine the look on her face when I told her!

She got upset and left. I thought she was overreacting. It didn't seem like such a big deal, right? My ex was just calling to check up on me, and we weren't getting back together or anything. I became immediately defensive, and I dug in my heels to plead my case. But Sharie explained her jealousy to me the next day.

"It's not that I don't trust you. That's not the point. I just don't want always to wonder if some girl you used to date might just randomly call you after we're married. **I am jealous for you because I love you.** If we're going to commit our lives to each other, then it's got to be exclusive."

We can learn something about God's jealousy from this story. Of course, lots of jealous people are just insecure. But God's jealousy for you is based on His desire to protect you and provide for you and love you as no one else can. He isn't jealous of your love for your family or your friends, your kids or your parents. **He is jealous of the love you have for anyone**

or anything else that replaces your love for Him as Lord. Just as I would be jealous if another man attempted to take my wife from me, Jesus is jealous when anything attempts to pull you away from Him as the Lord of your life.

He is jealous for you for your own good. His jealousy is good for you, like me protecting my son from burning himself on the motorcycle or my wife protecting our marriage from old girlfriends calling to check on me. He loves you too much to watch you ruin your life by ignoring Him and choosing another Lord.

A Firm Foundation

We lived in a house on a huge hill overlooking a creek on one side and the Broad River on the other. It's a pretty spot for a house. The backyard has an old settlement graveyard with five gravestones and a rock wall around it. The people who originally settled this property in the late 1700s thought the hill was a pretty spot, too, so they built their first house here, on this spot. But that house is long gone.

For many reasons our house will probably last a lot longer than that original log cabin. But the most important thing about this house that my family and I live in is the foundation. It's the basis for the whole thing. The kitchen, the bedrooms, my office, the upstairs, and the den all put their full weight on the foundation.

Before they put in the plumbing or the electricity or walls of our house, they dug deep into the ground and poured concrete. Solid, thick concrete. I was here watching them dig the huge hole with their tractors. I decided to do something that was both symbolic and significant.

I went to my truck and took out a little green Gideons New Testament. I waited until the work crew left for the day. I knew the concrete truck was coming the next morning, so I took that New Testament with me as I climbed down in the hole where the foundation would be poured. I read several passages out loud; then I prayed and dedicated our new home to Jesus. When I finished, I dug a little hole inside that huge hole, and I buried the Bible there. I was making a statement. I was saying: "Jesus, You are Lord of this family, and You are Lord of this house. Our home belongs to You. We will stand on Your truth, and we will live according to Your Word. You are our Foundation, and we will not be moved when we stand on You."

The next day they poured the concrete, and now an entire house stands on top of that foundation. If the foundation is faulty, the house will fall. If the foundation is deep, the house will stand.

I'm spending time laying this foundation here at the beginning of this book because this is what we build the whole *True Love Project* on. Once you've dug deep into the issue of who calls the shots, it's easier to know where you stand on what love is, who you are becoming, what kind of person you will date, who you want to marry, and what you will and won't do sexually before marriage.

If you get the foundation right, the house will stand steadfast. If the foundation is wrong, the house will begin to crumble and will eventually fall.

Who Is Your Lord?

The foundation for the *True Love Project* is an issue of ownership. It's about who's in charge of your life. Either Jesus is Lord or you are Lord. You're not big enough or strong enough or smart enough to be Lord, but Jesus is.

> He is the image of the invisible God, the firstborn over all creation. For everything was created by Him, in heaven and on earth, the visible and the invisible, whether thrones or dominions or rulers or authorities—all things have been created through Him and for Him. He is before all things, and by Him all things hold together. He is also the head of the body, the church; He is the beginning, the firstborn from the dead, so that He might come to have first place in everything. For God was pleased to have all His fullness dwell in Him, and through Him to reconcile everything to Himself by making peace through

the blood of His cross—whether things on earth or things in heaven. (Colossians 1:15–20)

It's hard to think of a more qualified candidate to be our Lord, to direct our lives, to trust with our relationships. When we consider the enormity of Jesus—His wisdom, His power, and His everlasting love for us—it seems silly to consider any other candidates as the true Lord of our lives.

Faith and Sacrifice

This is how your pursuit of purity begins—by faith.

Choose to trust God over and above your cravings. Believe that He wants to give you something, not take something away from you. He wants to give you abundant life and joy and real pleasure, the kind you find in a lifelong committed marriage. He wants to spare you from the heartache and heartbreak of sexual sin, the guilt and shame and regret that stick around long after the thrill is over.

If we'll just have the faith, Jesus has already made the sacrifice. And when we have faith in His sacrifice, we choose to model a life of sacrifice. Not only our relationships but also our entire lives are saved when we put our faith in Him.

Paul explained it to a group of Christians in Ephesus like this: "For you are saved by grace through faith, and this is not from yourselves; it is God's gift—not from works, so that no one can boast. For we are His creation, created in Christ Jesus for good works, which God prepared ahead of time so that we should walk in them" (Ephesians 2:8–10).

God's grace alone saves us, and our faith in Jesus is the means of receiving that grace. But that's only the beginning. A new person emerges as a result of this transformation, and awaiting us in our new journey of faith are "good works" God has prepared for us to do. He wants us to exercise our faith in Christ, not sit on it. We put that faith to work by doing things that model a life of sacrifice to the outside world. So our faith in His sacrifice naturally leads us into a life of sacrifice.

Our salvation is received, not achieved. We don't work for it. We don't earn it. We don't deserve it. It is a free gift that is offered to us—the true definition of grace. Jesus achieved our salvation; we receive our salvation.

When we have faith in the sacrifice Jesus made for us on the cross, we believe He alone can save us and satisfy us. We put complete trust in His words and in His work. We lay our lives down and put our lives in His hands. We have faith He will do what He said when He promised His followers He would prepare a place for them for all eternity in His presence. According to these words from Jesus, we're not really sacrificing anything of value when we lay our lives down and become His disciples. On the contrary, we gain so much more!

Don't think for a minute that sacrificing something like your desire for sex means you will never have the thing you want so bad. Have faith! Believe in God's promises! The endgame is not having sex (although it can be fantastic when you're married, trust me). The endgame is belonging to Jesus and being with Him forever in a place He has prepared for you.

> Your heart must not be troubled. Believe in God; believe also in Me. In My Father's house are many dwelling places; if not, I would have told you. I am going away to prepare a place for you. If I go away and prepare a place for you, I will come back and receive you to Myself, so that where I am you may be also. You know the way to where I am going. (John 14:1–4)

Our faith in His sacrifice leads us to live a life of sacrifice. Because He loved us and modeled what true sacrifice is, we follow His example; and as the Holy Spirit empowers us, we sacrifice our lives for Christ and for our brothers and sisters.

John, one of Jesus' disciples and His closest friend, understood this reality; and he instructs Christians to do the same in one of his letters in the New Testament: "This is how we have come to know love: He laid down His life for us. We should also lay down our lives for our brothers. If anyone has this world's goods and sees his brother in need but closes his eyes to his need—how can God's love reside in him? Little children, we must not love with word or speech, but with truth and action" (1 John 3:16–18).

True faith in Jesus leads to a life of compassion, care, humility, and sacrifice. It's impossible to know Jesus and not be ready and willing to sacrifice, or give up, everything to Him, proving our faith by our deeds.

Remember, this relationship thing—this *life* thing—is all about lordship or ownership. If Jesus is Lord, then He calls the shots; He owns what happens in your life. He asks you to receive His salvation by faith and sacrifice your own desires to Him as a result of believing in Him. When you do this, you enter a new part of God's story. You are no longer a mere sinner in need of redemption; you become a powerful tool infused with the Spirit of God, ready to be an agent of redemption for others.

When you begin to enter a deep understanding of what Jesus saved you from and how He wants you to live, it's easier to sacrifice your sexual desires and emotional urges to Christ by submitting to His lordship and leadership. He doesn't ask you to sacrifice something that would have been good for you in order to replace it with something bad for you. He would be a bad god if He did.

When the Bible reveals to us God's rules and boundaries governing relationships and love and sex, God's motive isn't to hurt you by asking you to sacrifice a good thing. And you don't have to sacrifice these desires forever. The time will come when your natural hunger for love and intimacy can be fully met without shame or guilt or fear.

God put those desires in you for a reason, and He will allow you to fulfill those desires—not just once but over and over for years and years—when you are ready and the time is right. If you refuse to sacrifice those desires now and instead choose to plow ahead in your pursuit of pleasure, it won't last, and you will pay a serious price (more on that later). But if you will sacrifice your momentary craving for sex and security, trusting that Jesus knows best, you can have the real thing later. And it will be better than you ever imagined.

So Who *Is* Lord of Your Life?

This decision is an important one, an urgent one. The rules and examples you choose to follow, the lord you choose for your life, are all laying the foundation for the rest of your life. Starting right now. In this very moment.

The awesome thing about choosing Jesus is that your new life starts right then, in that moment. Any past decisions, any crooked, weak structures you have built in your past are torn down, forgotten. And any new decisions, your new life, is built firmly on the foundation of the all-powerful, grace-filled Creator of the universe.

So when it comes to relationships, to true love, to making decisions that will undoubtedly affect the rest of your life, there really is only one candidate as the Lord and Owner of your life.

In choosing Him, you choose the truest love there is in this life . . . and ever after.

> "Choose for yourselves this day whom you will serve. . . . But as for me and my house, we will serve the LORD." (Joshua 24:15 NKJV)

True Talk

1. It's time to lay the foundation for the rest of your life. Who is your lord?

2. Do you think you're fully qualified to be the lord of your life? Explain.

3. Based on your everyday actions, how you spend your time and your money, and where you put your best efforts, would your friends and family agree with your answer to question 1?

4. What are some things you could do to show the world who is truly the Lord of your life?

CHAPTER 3

The Bible on Sex

God blessed them, and God said to them, "Be fruitful, multiply, fill the earth, and subdue it.

—Genesis 1:28

Many young people—and even adults—tend to view sex in one of two ways:

1. **Sex is god.**
2. **Sex is gross.**

The first perspective places sex (and the way sex makes you feel) as the centerpiece of your life. It's the ultimate goal. The big score. It becomes your driving force. You think about it constantly. It rules every thought while waking *and* sleeping. You size up people you meet as potential sex partners. You can't stop fantasizing about it. When you can't have it with a real person, you watch other people do it online. You text risqué photos of yourself and view them in return. You will use sex to keep a person (or people) in your life. You admit that you jump into it too fast in relationships, but it just happens before you know it.

Maybe you feel bad that you're so obsessive about it. Perhaps you've even tried to dial back a little bit or stop altogether. But it has such a tight grip on your mind and body that you can't stop. You can't control it because it controls you. You occasionally wonder if it will eventually hurt you or even ruin your life.

For you sex is god, and the result is sexual obsession.

The second perspective is equally destructive. It places sex in a category of shameful and nasty things that make you feel yucky. The mere mention of sex puts you on edge. You hate it when other people talk about it, whether in the context of a one-night stand or a married person speaking of it in respectful and joyful terms. You can't understand how anyone could enjoy sex because it seems so disgusting. You've wondered why you have such an adverse reaction to the subject. Or maybe you're fully aware of the root of the problem. It could go back to your childhood or something that happened six months ago. Maybe you were sexually abused. Or raped. Or manipulated. Or maybe you willingly entered into a sexual event or relationship that you deeply regret to this day. You wish you had never started messing around sexually. Or you hope you never have to.

For you sex is gross, and the result is sexual confusion.

These are the extremes. It doesn't mean you fit neatly into one of these categories. However, as our culture becomes more and more accepting of the public display of every kind of sexual perversion and deviance and sexual images flood our airwaves and our screens, our consciences are filled with competing voices and desires as our innocence gives way to sexual confusion and obsession. I pray that you are the exception to this rule.

The fact is simple: for hundreds of millions of people, sex really is god or gross. They live in sexual obsession or sexual confusion. But it doesn't have to be that way. It wasn't intended to be that way.

We need to explore a better way to view sex, beyond these destructive extremes. Let's dig deeper into the emotional, physical, psychological, and spiritual dimensions of sexuality and see how it affects the body and the brain. I believe you will be enlightened as God shines light on this powerful subject. I also think you'll be blown away to learn some things about how your body and brain work together, designed by God, to enjoy sexual intimacy in its proper context. Your sexuality is a part of your story, and your story is part of God's story. It matters.

Two New Perspectives

Is there a better way to think about sex than "god" and "gross"?

Thankfully, yes. I suggest that you replace these two words and the extreme perspectives they represent with two better words, healthy words, balanced words.

1. **Sex is a gift.**
2. **Sex is good.**

My Wake-up Call

I can remember with vivid clarity when I began to "wake up" to my inner sexual desires as a fifth and sixth grader. Those two years felt like an emotional and physical tornado for my mind and body. I began developing physically earlier than my friends. So I had facial hair and muscles before any of my friends did. Yeah, I sort of felt like a freak, but I also liked it. I was self-conscious enough to be embarrassed when I had to change clothes in the locker room for PE but proud enough that I cut all the sleeves off my T-shirts to parade my new armpit hair around school. It was a tumultuous time.

I also did a full reversal in the way I thought about girls. Until puberty I had placed girls in a category along with cats, math, and clowns: they were confusing, weird, and scary. But around age twelve, I noticed myself noticing them. Like,

THE BIBLE ON SEX

really *noticing* them. Like, I wanted to kiss them, hug them, hold their hands, or sit beside them at lunch. I wanted them to notice me for the first time too. So, of course, I started doing obnoxious things to get their attention.

One of many that I won't soon forget is my attempt to throw a curve ball in gym class to impress the girl I liked. I missed my target—the guy with the glove—and hit the basketball backboard, which shattered into four million pieces and cost me $1,500 to replace. All for the attention of a girl . . . who ended up dating my *former* best friend.

During this middle-school metamorphosis my opinion of girls dramatically changed. They were no longer gross. They were good. Very good!

At that time a neighbor of mine introduced me to a few pages he had torn out of one of his dad's *Playboy* magazines. (I'm sure his dad didn't notice. *Right?*) We looked at them in the woods deep inside the fort we'd built as an escape from the Russians when they invaded America. The magazine's pictures were what they used to call "soft porn," basically women with their clothes off, not doing anything with anybody but posing nude for pictures.

The first time I saw a naked woman on one of those pages was like an out-of-body experience. Because of the huge amounts of testosterone and adrenaline churning inside of me, my body was rapidly morphing from a boy into a man. I was waking up not only to the reality of sex but also to my own physical body. I suddenly had urges. I would see women on those pages and automatically want to have sex with them—even before I knew how to have sex.

My parents never had the sex talk with me. I figured it out on my own. We lived on a farm. I put two and two together. . . . You understand.

I was twelve and curious. My body was changing. My desires were changing. I had seen what a woman looked like under her clothes, and I began to think about and dream about girls. In the span of a few months, I went from playing army in the woods with my friends to fantasizing about making out with women. I stopped playing with G.I. Joe action figures and began dreaming of new action figures, the female kind, and my thoughts became a playground for fantasies. But it wasn't just sex I wanted. I vividly recall imagining having a family, being a dad to my children, and being married with a job. I was changing fast!

I Want It, But I Fear It

I was raised in a traditional church in a rural, conservative culture in the deep South. My parents were simple people who loved Christ with their whole hearts. They didn't tolerate foolishness and were faithful to instruct me in what the Bible said on all subjects.

I knew it was wrong to look at centerfolds from *Playboy* magazines. The same friend who introduced me to those had a VCR, too, and his parents were clueless to the kinds of movies he rented. My conscience was convicted every time I'd see some skin in a movie. I knew it was sinful to lust after girls, and even though I wasn't yet a Christian, my parents had instilled a Christian worldview in me so I knew right from wrong.

If you had asked me at that point to write you a book about purity, it would've gone more like this:

> Sex is horrible and nasty and disgusting. You could get AIDS. You could get the crabs. You could get gonorrhea or syphilis. You could get cervical cancer. And when you have sex with someone, you're also having sex with everyone they've ever had sex with. Isn't that awful? It will ruin your life and destroy your future. So save it for your husband or wife. The End

The one thing I lacked was any sort of reference point for what was happening to me sexually. I knew sex was a sin outside of marriage. I knew it caused people to catch diseases. It also led to babies, which I was in no way ready for. So I had two competing emotions inside my body at all times: the overwhelming urge to have sex and the crippling fear of what sex would do to me. I wanted it, and I was afraid of it.

When I wanted to be with a girl or when I dreamed about getting married and having sex on my honeymoon, I automatically felt condemned. It was torture! How could I want something so much that was evidently so bad for me?

Of course, I didn't know everything I needed to know. How could I? I was in sixth grade. It would take me years to see that sex wasn't created by Satan to hurt me. It was created by God as a gift to me. It took a while, but I eventually began to see the light. I began to understand that sex is a good gift given to us by a good God who intentionally created sex as a means of pleasure and procreation.

Sex Is a Gift

The word *gift* assumes a giver. Sexual intimacy was engineered by God as a gift to His children: the means of reproducing human life as well as a way to give and receive physical pleasure, while mirroring spiritual and emotional oneness in a marriage. And if sex is a gift to us, we could also assume that we'll be receiving that gift one day. Right?

Only God could think of something so good. Sir Isaac Newton once said that the opposable thumb alone was proof of the existence of God. I say that sex alone proves the existence of God. We can go all the way back to the beginning of our story and see that God instigated the relationship between the first man and woman. In fact, one of the first physical gifts God gave Adam was the gift of a mate. "Then the LORD God said, 'It is not good for the man to be alone. I will make a helper as his complement. . . . So the LORD God caused a deep sleep to come over the man, and he slept. God took one of his ribs and closed the flesh at that place. Then the LORD God made the rib He had taken from the man into a woman and brought her to the man. And the man said: This one, at last, is bone of my bone and flesh of my flesh; this one will be called "woman," for she was taken from man'" (Genesis 2:18, 21–23).

I've always imagined the scene when Adam woke up from his nap and Eve was standing before him. Adam's first reaction was to acknowledge the attraction he felt for the woman as well as the strong draw he felt toward her physically. Make no mistake; he uses tangible physical terms to describe their kinship and connection: "bone of my bone and flesh of my flesh." An immediate, irreversible physical connection existed between our original ancestors, and it was placed there by God Himself, on purpose. So you're not weird when you feel that same attraction. You're simply operating as God designed you. This attraction ultimately leads to a commitment. It leads to a relationship based on a covenant that the man and woman make to one another before God.

We call it marriage, God's original design for relationships: one man and one woman for life. Or as Genesis 2:24 puts it, "This is why a man leaves his father and mother and bonds with his wife, and they become one flesh."

Notice how the marriage relationship is exclusive. The man must "leave" his father and mother. He must mature, he must grow up, and he must become a man who is willing to leave all other relationships for the sake of the relationship with his wife. Marriage is, by nature, a relationship reserved for only two people. Then the husband and wife are able to experience a closeness that only exists in marriage. They actually become one flesh. This kind of strong language isn't used in the Bible to describe parents and their kids or the relationship between friends. And it isn't used to describe a sexual relationship between two men or between two women. It's only used to describe marriage between a man and a woman.

How does this happen? **How can two unique individuals become one flesh? It happens through the promise and covenant the two make to choose the marriage relationship as the primary commitment to another human being.** It is solidified when husband and wife are united. That uniting leads to their becoming one flesh. This is sexual intercourse. This is sexual intimacy. This is the ultimate act of love and trust and vulnerability two people can experience. And it's so intrinsically strong that it cements a bond between the man and the woman that ties them together both physically and emotionally. The ability to become one flesh is even reflected in God's design of the human body. Our anatomy is a sign and a symbol of God's desire for man and woman to make love, to feel attraction and desire, and to fulfill one another's craving for intimacy.

The best part of this original narrative where God brings Adam his first gift is how Adam and Eve related to each other after God introduced them. Notice their interaction in this short verse: "Both the man and his wife were naked, yet felt no shame" (Genesis 2:25).

It is clearly suggesting they enjoyed each other, particularly their bodies. The man felt no insecurity about being naked in front of his wife. The wife felt no shame about the appearance of her body in front of her husband. And what do you think they did after they realized they were naked? They had sex! They experienced the pleasure they could give each other. It was guilt-free. It was shame-free. It was sin-free. Just as God intended it to be.

God engineered those first two human bodies to go together. They were vastly different in anatomy yet undeniably attractive to each other. Even the physical body parts themselves fit perfectly with each other, as they still do, allowing the woman and the man to experience the full measure of joy during sex as well as the fulfillment of creating children, giving birth to them, and raising them to adulthood.

The Genesis account helps us to recognize the intricacies of the human bodies God created and the innate desires He placed in those two original prototypes. It makes me pause and worship God for this beautiful gift He graciously allows us to enjoy! And I do enjoy it, every bit of it, every second of it. More than just the act itself, I enjoy the company of my wife. I revel in the differences that are so apparent between the two of us. I love the things about her that don't naturally make sense to me. I love the long walks, the hard conversations, the seasons of doubt and fear and discouragement, and the things she teaches me about myself. What a gift!

Sex Is Good

Sex came from God, and God gives good things to His children. Sex is powerful, intimate, transformative, and exhilarating. It involves every aspect of a person's mind, heart, and body. It requires trust, tenderness, patience, and understanding. Really, something as wonderful and satisfying as sex with your spouse could have only been thought up by someone as smart as God.

The church father Augustine said, "Marriage, therefore, is a good in all the things which are proper to the married state. And these are three: it is the ordained means of procreation, it is the guarantee of chastity, it is the bond of union." Since the earliest days of the church, Christians have celebrated the goodness of sex when it is enjoyed in a covenant of marriage.

Even though the church has historically agreed that sex is reserved for the marriage relationship, it has not always clearly explained the complex opinions and views on sex, celibacy, forgiveness, and restoration. Much of the conversation about sex in Christian circles leaves one with the impression that sex is bad, nasty, gross, sinful, disgusting, and regrettable. Nothing could be further from the truth. As we've already seen, God instigated sex in the institution of marriage, even commanding Adam and Eve to come together physically. Genesis 1:28 says, "God blessed them, and God said to them, 'Be fruitful, multiply, fill the earth, and subdue it.'"

> The modern sexual revolution finds the idea of abstinence from sex til marriage to be so unrealistic as to be ludicrous. . . . Yet despite the contemporary incredulity, this has been the unquestioned, uniform teaching of not only one but all of the Christian churches—Orthodox, Catholic, and Protestant.
> —Timothy Keller, *The Meaning of Marriage*[1]

Notice the language. It was a *blessing* for God to give them the ability to have sex as well as a means of filling the earth with more human beings who would, in turn, continue to bear the fruit of marriage.

Don't miss this: sex within a godly marriage is a blessing.

It naturally creates more people, and each person is God's image bearer.

It is good.

Good for What?

God uses sexual intimacy between a husband and wife for many purposes, but here are three in particular.

1. Procreation. Spoiler alert: The stork doesn't really bring babies. Creating another human life takes a man and a woman, complete with their male and female anatomies. Sex is the physical act God uses to populate the earth with people He loves. Furthermore, each of us is wired to connect with other humans in relationships, so sex is necessary for the flourishing of humanity as well as the continuation of the human race. Every human, in spite of his sinful nature, also bears the image of God and can be redeemed and restored to a right relationship with God through faith in Christ.

2. Recreation. The bedroom in a marriage can become a playground for adults when there is mutual trust, patience, and understanding. Sharie and I make love without guilt or shame because we know and trust each other. It's often playful and silly. We laugh and cut up and don't take ourselves as seriously as we did at first. As a result, we look forward to our special times and have fun leading up to those moments.

It's more enjoyable than water skiing, hiking, swimming, or any of the other activities we do together for recreation. It's a small part of our marriage, but it's a powerful part nonetheless.

3. Communication. Sex forces a married couple to be attentive to the needs and feelings of each other. It pushes you to embrace the awkwardness of talking about something so intimate with your partner, owning up to what you like and don't like before, during, and after sex. It also allows you to figure out ways to pursue each other outside the bedroom, saying and doing things for each other that create mutual feelings of affection and care. Acts of service and submission in all other areas of the marriage often lead to more sexual intimacy as trust and communication increase. We've learned to communicate verbally and nonverbally, with smiles and winks and funny looks, with acts of service like washing dishes or cooking a meal together.

So for us sex is a good gift that is waiting for us at the finish line of a thousand conversations, a hundred struggles, and a dozen misunderstandings. We learn to listen, to extend grace patiently, and to try to understand each other. Because sex is essentially an act of communication, the more struggles we weather and the more valleys we travel through, the more intimately we express our love for each other, and sex is the physical manifestation of that emotional and spiritual bond. Sex is not our primary means of communicating our affections for each other. Rather, it is the by-product of loving each other daily and serving each other faithfully.

Sex Is Good, but Is It Always Great?

So we've moved away from the two extremes of "sex is god" and "sex is gross." We see that it is not a divine thing to be worshipped. Neither is it a disgusting thing to be shunned. Sex is a gift, and sex is good. It brings physical and emotional pleasure, it serves a practical purpose in re-populating the planet, and it was created by God for us.

So does that mean that sex must be great?

If God made it and it is good, then shouldn't we expect it to be something that takes our breath away every time we experience it?

I get it. I do.

The thought process goes something like this: *If I am going to submit myself to Jesus and follow His plan for my life, then I am surrendering my sexual desires to His lordship. So if I am going to live by His expectations, resisting temptation and waiting until marriage to experience sexual intimacy, then it better be worth the wait! I'm not giving up sexual urges for no reason; I want it to be awesome when it finally happens, and I better not be disappointed.*

OK, so you would never actually say that to God, but this seems to be the attitude many Christians have about sex once they pledge to remain abstinent until marriage. Is this a healthy way to anticipate the joy of sex, though? Is there a guarantee that waiting until marriage will ensure you the best sex possible? And if sex isn't immediately awesome, does that mean you made the wrong decision by choosing chastity and purity?

Although marriage and sex may seem a long way off, I would be doing you an injustice by not addressing this here and now. These are essential issues that plague many married couples, primarily because of the unrealistic expectations people smuggle into marriage.

Because sex is a powerful act that always affects (either positively or negatively) those who experience it, it would seem reasonable to assume that sex affects you after you're married as much as it does before you're married.

Once you've tied the knot, the power of sex in influencing your feelings and emotions increases exponentially, not only for you but also for your spouse. Both of you are taking the plunge into a promise; you're dedicating your lives to each other. You've spoken vows and entered into a covenant. You open yourself up completely and irreversibly to another person, and eventually the flaws and failures of both individuals have a head-on collision.

That collision of ideas does not exclude sex. It includes any past experiences, private fantasies, one-night stands, old college boyfriends, pornographic images stored in the brain, and what you hope you will feel in the bedroom with your spouse. This is true for the inexperienced virgin, the regretful playboy, and the victim of sexual abuse. Everyone brings his or her experiences and expectations into the marriage bedroom. *Everyone.*

And increasingly people have an unrealistic expectation of sexual bliss that is filled with flames and fireworks. They want to have hot, passionate sex every time they make love. They want explosions of pleasure. Hollywood bodies and climactic scenes from chick flicks have filled the brain. Many have secretly watched scenes online they want to play out in real life. All of these factors on the front end of a marriage create complications in the bedroom and lead to sexual frustration and disappointment for those who dreamed of having great sex from the beginning.

Frankly, you are going to be disappointed with sex at some point—even if you're a strong Christian, even if you've healed from past mistakes, and even if you were a virgin on your wedding day.

Don't misunderstand me: sex is wonderful and brings amazing amounts of pleasure and intimacy in the marriage relationship. But the reason you should practice chastity and purity before marriage is *not* because it guarantees you a lifetime of great sex. **You practice sexual purity because you belong to Jesus, because your body is now His dwelling place and He is using your life as a witness to the world that His**

gospel is true and His kingdom is coming. If that's not your motivation for submitting your sexuality to God's standards of holiness, then you will bail out on purity as soon as you get frustrated or disappointed, even in your marriage. And you will feel frustrated. I can guarantee that.

This reality came crashing down on me one day when I saw a good friend at church who was a newlywed. He confronted me angrily.

"It was all a lie! I saved myself for marriage. I could have had lots of sex, but I waited because everyone kept saying, 'True love waits!' Just so you know: it was a mistake. It's just not working for us. We didn't even have sex on our honeymoon! Is that how God rewards me for waiting until marriage?"

He was livid, and he felt like he had been tricked.

Of course, he was frustrated because he had only been anticipating great sex. He hadn't prepared himself for the self-giving, sacrificial love a marriage demands. Issues of abuse would also later come to light in their marriage. But the point remains: there is no guarantee.

So . . . no, the sex won't always be great. It may not even be there at all. A terrible accident, a disease, or cancer could end a couple's sex life. And if sex or romance is all you're looking for in life, you will be devastated when the unexpected realities of life occur. But if you're yielded to Jesus and your desire is to love your mate unconditionally and serve your spouse without expectations, the Holy Spirit will guide you through those seasons of struggle and disappointment.

The Source of the Mind-set

Where exactly do we get these unrealistic ideas about having perfect sex every time? Here are the primary sources that feed us these silly notions.

The Dominant Culture

America is obsessed with sex. Television, movies, and social media incessantly fill our eyes and our minds with images and messages about sexuality.

- One-third of all online downloads are porn.
- Seventy percent of all TV shows marketed to teenagers are about sex.
- Porn is a $15 billion business annually.
- Forty-three percent of Internet users look at porn regularly.
- The average age of first exposure to online porn is eleven.
- Child porn generates $3 billion every year.[2]

And on a personal note, just this week as I was standing in line at the grocery store, I read these captions on magazine covers, at eye level with my seven and ten-year-old sons:

- "Great Sex Every Time"
- "Bedroom Tricks to Make Your Man Scream"

- "10 Naughty New Positions You've Never Tried"
- "Tease Him Before You Please Him"

I don't think anyone in their right mind would argue that our culture wants you sexually aroused all the time. It's the air we all breathe in America.

The Evangelical Church

Unfortunately, much of the sexual disappointment married couples face can be traced back to the influence of the church they attended or the books they read in preparation for tying the knot. The dominant message of the past twenty-five years among evangelicals regarding sex has been incomplete at best and harmful at worst. Popular books and numerous leaders, with a godly desire to address sexuality from a Christian perspective, have communicated ideas that don't always play out as they are predicted.

Here are a few:

- If you have sex before you get married, you will feel dirty as soon as you're done.
- If you wait to have sex on your honeymoon, it will be the best feeling you've ever had.
- If you're not a virgin, just pray and ask God to forgive you, and it will be just like the "first time" again when you have sex with your husband or wife.

- If you wait until your wedding night, you will instinctively know what to do; it will be completely natural.
- Waiting until you're married guarantees passionate sex and physical satisfaction every time.

Ask any Christian couple who has been married for more than six months, and they will confirm that these are simply not true. Sex is not an event to bring you pleasure. It's the union of two bodies and two souls within a lifelong covenant, and it's not always easy or satisfying. This is reality.

The Silence of Leaders and Parents

When moms and dads and pastors and leaders don't talk honestly with those they lead about sexuality, a vacuum is created; and it is filled with other voices that preach their own gospel of sexual freedom, deviance, and perversion.

But it's a fact that:

- When a parent expresses disapproval of their child having sex, they are less likely to engage in sexual activity.[3]
- Teenagers who talk to their parents before having sex have fewer sex partners and wait longer to begin having sex.[4]
- When parents instruct their teenagers about sex through ongoing conversation, the vast majority of

those teenagers will rely on their parents, not their friends or the media, for guidance and information about sex.[5]

As awkward as it may seem, it really helps to talk to your parents or other supportive adults about what you're thinking and feeling about your relationships. They can help you stay committed to your path and help you set realistic expectations.

Where you get your information about sex will make all of the difference in how your expectations are shaped and how your relationships are formed. We'll do what we can within the pages of this book, but your journey will require so much more than that. If Jesus is Lord of your life, stick to God's design for relationships and seek out what the Bible has to say about sex. Seek out the advice of Christian adults— believe it or not, we've been there!

We need to have frequent, honest conversations about sex, love, and romance. The reality is as plain as dirt: it takes the grace of God and a lifetime of hard work to have healthy relationships where both people serve each other and where sex can be experienced as God designed it.

It may seem like a lifetime away, but it can happen, and the preparation starts today.

True Talk

1. What does the Bible say about sex and marriage?

2. Why do you think God designed sex to be limited to marriage between a man and a woman?

3. List some views of sex that society has presented to you.

4. Now go through the Bible and find out what God has to say about each of those views.

CHAPTER 4

Your Heart Matters

Guard your heart above all else, for it is the source of life.

— Proverbs 4:23

You cannot be sexually or romantically intimate with another person without involving your heart.

Think about how we describe our feelings for another person. We always place our heart at the center of the conversation. We say things like:

"I love you with all my heart."

"I don't know what's going on in my heart right now."

"Every time I see him, my heart races!"

"She broke my heart."

"I know in my heart that this is right."

"I gave him my heart, and look what he did to me!"

Isn't it interesting how we intuitively talk about love in regard to how it feels "in our hearts"? And isn't it fascinating that our hearts are always central to the feelings and emotions we associate with falling in love, getting hurt, being disappointed, or feeling betrayed? How odd is it that we connect the most wonderful emotion with a three-pound muscle inside our chest that pumps blood through our bodies?

We are not the first ones to talk or think in these terms, however. Even a brief glance at Scripture proves God created us in such a unique way that we connect with other people emotionally and physically with our "hearts." We are even commanded by Jesus Himself to love God with "all of our heart."

"Love the Lord your God with all your heart, with all your soul, and with all your mind." (Matthew 22:37)

"For where your treasure is, there your heart will be also." (Matthew 6:21)

"Take delight in the Lord, and He will give you your heart's desires." (Psalm 37:4)

"Guard your heart above all else, for it is the source of life." (Proverbs 4:23)

Obviously the heart is more than the muscle that pumps your blood, and based on the passages above, we're not the only ones who think so. The heart is the center of all human affection, the storehouse of all human emotion. It represents the "inner person" who needs and yearns for love and affection. It's that internal part of you that actually responds to other humans, feels attraction, senses attachment, suffers rejection, and longs for the unconditional love and acceptance of others. The heart is the place where we experience the love of God, where we choose to esteem and honor Him above all things, and where we give Him the highest place in our lives. In our hearts we set apart Christ as Lord, allowing Him to take the place we selfishly desire for ourselves.

The heart is sensitive, tender, and fragile. Proverbs 4:23 goes so far as to say that your heart is the very "source of life." That is why we are instructed to guard it with great care. Your heart retains memories long forgotten by the mind, and some of them make absolutely no sense.

I can still remember with absolute clarity a blow to my heart from my sophomore year in college. I met this girl on the first day of classes and felt an immediate chemistry between us. We went on a few dates, and we just clicked. We both felt called to ministry and had similar desires for the future. But she had an ex-boyfriend back home that she was still hung up on. I asked her to end things with him once and for all. I still remember the conversation vividly.

"I can't continue pursuing you until you choose which one of us you really want to be with. It's too hard for me to keep wondering which one of us you really like. I feel like my heart is being torn in half."

I was trying to guard my heart because the things it was feeling were keeping me up at night with anxiety and fear. I couldn't eat or sleep. All I thought about all day was her, wondering if she would pick me over him or if she would break my heart.

Her response was, "Clayton, I want you to know that you are the only man in my heart. I would never hurt you. I want to be with you and no one else."

Those simple words calmed down the raging emotions inside my heart. A simple promise of exclusive affection from her set me at ease. But that feeling was short-lived. Just a few weeks later, she let me know that she had gone home for the weekend and went out with her ex-boyfriend.

She said, "I began to feel for him again, things I hadn't felt in a long time. I can't deny what my heart felt. When I am with him, my heart loves him. But when I am with you, my heart loves you. I am completely torn and confused."

Because her heart was so volatile, my heart was volleyed back and forth in an egg toss until it eventually crashed to the ground in a broken, gooey mess. Don't you see how sensitive the heart really is? And don't you see how fickle and unpredictable it is too? The Bible warns us that without the transforming power of Jesus, we can never really trust our hearts.

Deceitful, Sick, and Confusing?

When we think about our hearts, we think of them as innocent and filled with love. When it comes to relationships, you've probably heard people say, "Just follow your heart," or "Trust your heart." But the Bible uses a few other words to describe the fascinating, complex nature of the home of our emotions and affections. And what it says may surprise you.

Jeremiah 17:9 says, "The heart is more deceitful than anything else, and incurable—who can understand it?" What? More deceitful than *anything else*? Not just sick but *incurable*? And the kicker: it's so confusing that no one really understands it! This can't be right!

But you know this verse is totally true. Think about the up-and-down nature of your own heart: the range of emotions you feel on any given day, the highs and lows of your relationships, and the confusion you feel about love and romance. Think about all the songs that have been written about breaking up, broken hearts, and betrayed promises. We would have no country music if it weren't for broken promises and broken hearts. How much money has Taylor Swift made off her ex-boyfriends alone?

You know your heart is unpredictable, sensitive, and tender. So doesn't it make sense that a romantic relationship, which exists in your heart, will affect your heart in deep and irreversible ways? And how much more will sex and physical intimacy affect your heart? God knows this better than we do. That's why God establishes guidelines for how you relate to other people, especially romantically and physically. It is for your protection, not your punishment.

When my children suffer, it hurts me. When God's children suffer, it hurts God. He hurts when we hurt because He loves us. He knows our hearts are wishy-washy and confusing and, if we follow them without any boundaries, they will lead us to emotional ruin. So in love God gives us parameters and rules to keep us from hurting ourselves and others. He allows us to do certain things, and other things He calls off-limits. He is helping us protect our hearts. But He gives us more than rules to follow—He gives us a new heart that He fills with His own Spirit, and, eventually, new desires.

So if all of this is true, you don't really have a lust problem. You don't really have a porn problem. You don't even really have a sex problem.

You have a heart problem.

Your heart, our hearts, are deceitful. Sick. Confused. To put it simply, the heart is sinful. It selfishly wants to be satisfied with its own desires at the expense of others. And until that heart is made new by the grace of Jesus Christ, it cannot be trusted.

This is a hard pill to swallow, I know. We don't like being told that our hearts are wicked and untrustworthy, even though we know down deep that it's the truth.

But it's not all bad news! There is hope: "For if our heart condemns us, God is greater than our heart, and knows all things" (1 John 3:20 NKJV). The power of the gospel can change our sick, deceitful hearts and make them brand-new. God can do this because He is greater, stronger, and more powerful than the crazy, confusing feelings our hearts experience on any given day.

Heart Problems

The period of time from 2002 to 2012 was the most difficult decade of my life. It all began with a simple little phrase my dad said to me one day on the phone after a visit to his doctor.

He had been feeling fatigued and irritable for over a year. His emotions were unpredictable. He would get upset about random things, lose his temper over minor issues, and feel panic and anxiety over the smallest things. After feeling tightness in his chest, he decided to have some tests run. When I picked up the phone to get the report, his words stuck like a dagger in my heart. "Son, I've got bad news. I knew something was wrong with me. I have a heart problem."

My father had been diagnosed with heart disease, largely a result of diabetes. For the next ten years, I witnessed the strongest man I'd ever known slowly waste away until he could no longer walk or even hold a cup in his hand. The heart disease ravished his body until it took him down. He suffered his fifth heart attack on a Thursday morning, and he died two days later. On Father's Day I would preach my own father's funeral.

Many times since that day in 2002, when I have struggled with lust or shame or sinful desires, I've remembered that conversation with my dad, and I've said to myself, "Clayton, you have a heart problem."

This is true for you. It's true for all of us.

Jesus' brother said so much in his short letter found in the New Testament. He understood that all sin and impurity first flow from the heart before showing up in our actions. "What is the source of wars and fights among you? Don't they come from the cravings that are at war within you? You desire and do not have. You murder and covet and cannot obtain. You fight and war. You do not have because you do not ask. You ask and don't receive because you ask with wrong motives, so that you may spend it on your evil desires" (James 4:1–3).

Doesn't this describe how you often feel? It makes so much sense when we realize our behavior isn't the issue. It's the sinful nature of the heart, and only God can cure it.

Each of us is a sinner. Nobody is exempt. We are all in the same boat. The Bible is clear. Romans 3:23 is explicit when Paul declares that we have all sinned and fallen short of the glory of God. He echoes this in Romans 6:23 when he plainly states that the result of our sin is death. This sounds like bad news, and indeed it is. But good news follows the bad news, and there is hope for you in your quest for purity and true love.

Paul goes on to say in Romans 6:23 that even though sin brings death, God offers the gift of eternal life through Jesus Christ. That is good news as you think about eternity. It means you won't live forever separated from God. But there is also good news in this life, in this world, while you're still alive here on this planet. "But thank God that, although you used to be slaves of sin, you obeyed from the heart that pattern of teaching you were transferred to, and having been liberated from sin, you became enslaved to righteousness. . . . So what fruit was produced then from the things you are now ashamed of? For the end of those things is death. But now, since you have been liberated from sin and have become enslaved to God, you have your fruit, which results in sanctification—and the end is eternal life!" (Romans 6:17–18, 21–22).

Isn't that beautiful? Isn't that powerful? Isn't that encouraging? Read that passage again and realize what the Bible is saying to you. Sin makes you a slave. It controls you and it takes from you. You never gain any benefit from living sinfully and selfishly. Sexual sin ultimately leaves you with shame and death. But Jesus can reverse the curse. He liberates from sin and offers you the benefits of holiness and eternal life.

Jesus is the cure for your heart problem. And your lust problem. And your shame problem. And your guilt problem. And your porn problem. And your sex problem. And ultimately your sin problem.

We Are All Sexual Sinners

We all like to imagine that we are way better than other people, especially all those "weird sexual perverts" we read about online or see on the news. But in one sense every single one of us is a sexual sinner. Before you begin to think that you aren't all that bad and that your heart is not as sick as some of your friends, you might want to read something Jesus had to say about the human heart, especially sexual sin: "You have heard that it was said, Do not commit adultery. But I tell you, everyone who looks at a woman to lust for her has already committed adultery with her in his heart" (Matthew 5:27–28).

Right there Jesus blows up any idea of self-righteousness. Until that moment the Pharisees, the pious religious leaders, probably felt pretty good about themselves. I'm sure they congratulated one another and looked sternly down their noses at the rest of the people because they had never participated in the physical act of sex with another man's wife. But Jesus surprises the crowd when He connects sexual sin to the human heart, not just the human body.

Imagine the Pharisees' response when Jesus told them if they had ever lusted after a woman, they had committed adultery with her in their heart! I've never met a man who didn't struggle with lustful thoughts or lustful looks. Not even a Pharisee could claim immunity to lust.

The Jews were accustomed to being led by the Pharisees and other groups of religious professionals like them. These leaders were always focusing on outer behavior, rigidly enforcing that people keep the law and live by hundreds of man-made rules. They had laws governing how to wash your hands before a meal, how far you could walk from your house on the Sabbath day, and whether you could eat an egg laid by a chicken on Saturday. (I am not making this stuff up.) But they ignored the place where sin starts. They never dealt with the heart. They just tried to control people's behavior.

Jesus, on the other hand, is always pointing our attention back inside. He wants us to focus on the engine, not the paint job. The *heart* is valued above all things because it's the engine that generates affection, desire, and worship. God sees the *heart*. The *heart* is where Christ lives.

He wants us to examine the source of all our desires. He points past the superficial rules of the Pharisees to remind us of the true source of sexual sin. He reminds us that simply looking at someone with sexual desire is destructive and hurtful. Even if you never act it out physically, the sin affects your heart.

It also offends the holiness of God.

Sin begins in the heart, and we are all sinners who need God's salvation and grace—from the most religious to the most rebellious.

What Is Off-Limits?

So you're probably wondering, *If even thinking about sex with someone outside of marriage is a sin, is everything completely off-limits? What about kissing? touching? kissing while touching?*

Whoa, there. Believe me, I understand. But first, before we can establish what is right and wrong sexually, a few things need to be understood.

1. God is the ultimate authority, and He alone ultimately decides and declares what is right and wrong, what is good and bad. As Creator of all things (including your body), He has the final say.

2. Remember, God does not declare certain things off-limits to hurt you or punish you but to help you and protect you. He loves you and only wants you to experience joy and love and happiness in a relationship with Him and with others.

3. God has revealed Himself fully and completely in Jesus Christ and through His Word, the Bible. All we need to know about salvation, faith, and practice we find in Scripture. Without the Word of God, we would not have a way to understand the story God began with creation and how we have a place in it.

4. God continues to reveal Himself to us through His Holy Spirit as He guides us, convicts us, comforts us, and transforms us into the image of Jesus Christ as His disciples.

To say that people today are confused about what is right and wrong when it comes to relationships and sex is an understatement. The definitions of *love, marriage, family,* and *commitment* are rapidly changing. And although our culture preaches a message of sexual freedom and liberty, we still intuitively know that certain things are inherently wrong. Our laws reflect this belief. Each of us knows that certain things are just wrong.

It is illegal for a thirty-five-year-old schoolteacher to seduce a fourteen-year-old student into a sexual relationship. It is illegal for a man to have five wives. It is illegal for adults to force children into prostitution. So please, don't fall for the lie, "Nothing is wrong as long as you feel good about it in your heart." Remember what we learned about our poor hearts? Still, we all know that certain things are sexually wrong, destructive, and sinful.

The real question is not about what we can and can't do. The primary question is whether you trust God and His Word.

Do you really believe that God knows best? That God loves you and wants the best for you? That God is smarter than you and He sees the future outcomes of your sin? If you don't really trust God's good intentions for you, then you'll have a hard time surrendering your sexual and romantic desires to Him. Who did you decide is lord of your life? If Jesus is Lord, then it is fitting that you submit to Him and all He has revealed in His Word concerning your body, sex, desires, and cravings for love and affection.

Nevertheless, people are always asking the wrong question when it comes to sexual purity. Here's a mercifully short list of the most common questions I'm asked regularly.

- How far is too far?
- Is sex before marriage a sin if we really love each other?
- I prayed about it in my heart, and I don't feel bad about it at all, so it must be OK. Right?

- I asked God to take away my desire, and He didn't, so it's not wrong, is it?
- What about making out, sleeping together, oral sex, or mutual masturbation? It's not intercourse, so is it OK?
- We know we're going to get married, so what's the difference in doing it now and waiting a few years to do it?

Each of these questions is asked from a wrong perspective. The heart behind questions like these is simply, How can I get what *I* want without the consequences of sin? And a heart with that motive cannot be trusted; it will most certainly lead you into sin, sooner rather than later, and you will suffer the long-reaching consequences.

So is there a better question to ask? Is there something better than asking, "What is off-limits?"

A Better Question

Let's try replacing "How far can I go before I sin?" with these:

- How holy can I be?
- What does the Bible have to say about this?
- How can I honor God with my heart and with my body?
- If I do this, will I feel guilty and ashamed afterward?

- Will I be embarrassed to tell my future spouse about this?
- Will doing this cause me conviction?
- Will I have to repent of this and ask God to forgive me?
- Is a small voice inside my heart telling me this is wrong?
- Will I regret this?
- Is this a violation of Scripture?

The real question goes back to lordship. If Jesus is your Lord, then you should ask, **"Will this bring glory and honor to Jesus?"**

If you're honest with yourself, this question will always clarify the situation you're in, no matter what the temptation is.

We've already seen that God has an intention and a design for sexuality. It starts at the beginning of God's story, all the way back in Genesis with Adam and Eve in the garden of Eden. But let's look at a few verses in the New Testament where God inspires Paul to give some instructions about sex. You'll notice that God hasn't changed His mind or His standards concerning sex. It is meant exclusively for one man and one woman in marriage. No exceptions.

Now in response to the matters you wrote about:
"It is good for a man not to have relations with

a woman." But because sexual immorality is so common, each man should have his own wife, and each woman should have her own husband. A husband should fulfill his marital responsibility to his wife, and likewise a wife to her husband. A wife does not have the right over her own body, but her husband does. In the same way, a husband does not have the right over his own body, but his wife does. Do not deprive one another sexually—except when you agree for a time, to devote yourselves to prayer. Then come together again; otherwise, Satan may tempt you because of your lack of self-control. (1 Corinthians 7:1–5)

The clear understanding is that sex belongs in marriage, not outside of it. It is an exclusive relationship between a man and a woman. Sex is expected and celebrated in marriage. The two partners explore and enjoy each other's bodies, and they are commended to offer their bodies to each other for pleasure. At times they may mutually choose to abstain from sex for various reasons, spiritually or practically, but eventually they should enter back into a physically intimate relationship because that is how God designed marriage and human bodies to work and function.

If this is God's design from the beginning to the end of Scripture, then certain things fall outside of God's design. Although all sexual sins may be forgiven by a loving and gracious God, that doesn't mean you have a license to deviate into sexual sin without pain and regret, even though you may repent and receive God's grace. In love and wisdom God declares certain sexual behaviors sinful, destructive, and off-limits:

- Sex before marriage, also called "fornication"
- Sex with someone outside of your own marriage, also called "adultery"
- Crude humor and sexually explicit joking
- Pornography, experimenting, and anything that causes lustful desires
- Homosexuality and sexual intimacy with the same gender
- Sex with more than one person (your spouse)
- Using sex as a tool for dominance, control, or intimidation
- Casual sexual intimacy for selfish gratification
- Any sexual activity that devalues the other person or ignores that person's integrity

Facts Are Our Friends

Of course, any time we're given a list of rules, as humans, our natural tendency is rebellion. And I get it: We want sex and romance, and we want to feel pleasure from it. We want to feel secure because of it, and we want to be able to walk

away from sex at any time unaffected by it. But this is physically, spiritually, and scientifically impossible. You can't have
sex with your body and not have sex with your soul. It's no
coincidence that scientific facts only reinforce the rules God
has given us.

Consider just a handful of the major findings of The
Medical Institute for Sexual Health. Joe McIlhaney, MD, and
Freda McKissic Bush, MD, spent years studying the physical effects of sexual activity on the human brain and body,
and they released their conclusive findings in the fascinating
book, *Hooked: New Science on How Casual Sex Is Affecting
Our Children*. Although our culture preaches a message of
sexual liberation that centers on individual freedom to do
anything and everything with anyone and everyone, the facts
tell us serious consequences follow when you act carelessly
with your sexuality.

> For instance:
> The younger teenagers are when they initiate
> sexual activity, the more sexual partners they
> will be likely to have by the time they are inter-
> viewed again in their twenties. Sexual behavior
> for this young group, once it has commenced,
> **appears almost compulsive**. This certainly corre-
> lates with neuroscientific findings that sex has an
> addictive effect on the brain[1] (emphasis added).

It appears that the most up-to-date research suggests that most humans are "designed" to be sexually monogamous with one mate for life. This information also shows that the further individuals deviate from this behavior, the more problems they encounter, be they STDs, non-marital pregnancy, or emotional problems, including damaged ability to develop healthy connectedness with others, including future spouses.[2]

The riskiest sexual situations by far are those that involve an increasing number of sexual partners with no commitment whatsoever. When individuals begin having sex with minimal or no commitment, it is often called "hooking up." A similar sexual relationship is often referred to as "friends with benefits," in which a couple decides to have sex whenever one or the other wants it but without any obligation, any promise of a future relationship, and without any intended emotion for each other. The one thing we know for sure is that such behavior is rampant among American young people.[3]

Some of you won't be surprised by these facts—you've already seen them playing out in the lives of your friends and the halls of your schools. And now you have just a sampling of the treasure trove of scientific data that backs up what we all know is true: sex is a real and powerful force, and it should be treated with great care and caution.

Sexual connection needs a spiritual covenant and an emotional commitment to make it work properly; otherwise it becomes a total catastrophe. That's the way it was designed from the beginning.

Brains, Bonds, and Chemicals

During physical intimacy, way more is going on inside the human body than getting butterflies in your stomach or experiencing an increased heart rate. Thousands upon thousands of chemical exchanges and explosions happen when two people experience romance and sexual intimacy. "When two people join physically, powerful neurohormones are released because of the sexual experience, making an impression on the synapses in their brains and hardwiring their bond. When they stay together for life, their bonding matures. This is a major factor that keeps them together, providing desire for intercourse, resulting in offspring, and assuring those offspring of a nurturing two-parent home in which to grow."[4]

Just as scientists have proven that sex is addictive and destructive outside of marriage, they have also proven that within marriage both the spouses and their children have the greatest chance to experience love, stability, and happiness.

Sexual activity floods the brain and the body with hormones and chemicals that lock in the memories of the feelings associated with that experience. Marriage is a healthy place for those memories and images. And it becomes pretty clear why you don't want a hardwired bond with several different people over the course of time.

How Does It Work?

You've probably heard a little bit about adrenaline, serotonin, estrogen, and testosterone. All of these chemicals and many more are actively involved in human sexuality. Recently experts have compiled data from studies that explain how and why sex affects us so radically. The findings are fascinating. They are also frightening.

Neurons are the primary cells in the brain. Each one of these neurons communicates through connections called *synapses*. A synapse is like an electronic signal, something like an e-mail or a text message. They are also similar to a muscle; if you use them, they grow stronger, but if you don't use them, they grow weaker.

The brain has more than 100 trillion synapse connections (more than all the Internet connections in the world combined), and each one of them communicates, sends, and stores all your feelings, desires, fears, wants, dislikes, thoughts, and memories. This is the part of the brain where habits are formed and broken. It's also how the brain experiences addiction.[5]

Your brain houses all the data sent and received regarding your life. When I download a song or a sermon, it's saved in "the cloud." Somewhere in a warehouse, Google and Apple and Facebook are storing all of my e-mails, my messages, my playlists, and my information. They never go away. And this is how your brain stores experiences, events, and memories. Especially when they are romantic and sexual.

Dopamine kick-starts these synapses. It is a messenger chemical that gives people a good, rewarding feeling when they do something exciting, and it floods the brain during sex, causing the synapses to fire, sending and receiving signals. This involuntary chemical reaction happens in the prefrontal cortex of the brain, the same area that's used to make important, complex decisions. This part of the brain is not fully developed until you are in your mid-twenties, but when you have sex at an early age, dopamine is released, the memory is locked in the brain, and you chemically crave that same pleasure. However, because the prefrontal cortex is not fully mature, you lack the ability to make wise decisions in light of the consequences of those actions. Meanwhile, the more sex you have, the more dopamine is released, and the more addicted to the feeling you become. You naturally crave more. It's quite literally a drug.[6]

Bonding and Monogamy

In females a "bonding" chemical called oxytocin is released during romantic physical contact and helps women build trust when they get close or intimate with a man. It is released regardless of the intent of the man she is having sex with. Whether he is her husband or a drunk frat boy, she will still have an unstoppable desire to bond with him after sex. This is the woman's chemical cement, and it works great if she's married to the guy she is physically intimate with. Otherwise, it's like ripping her heart out of a cement cast.

So many females admit to feeling sad, depressed, and unloved after they've experienced sexual intimacy with a man they're not married to, even if he says he loves her. It's a scientific reality: the body is created to connect for more than just sex, and when the sex is over, there's often a feeling of abandonment and loneliness resulting from oxytocin released in the brain.

This is markedly dangerous for younger girls in sexual relationships: "The adolescent girl who enters into a close relationship may therefore find herself, because of the normal effect of her brain hormones, desiring more physical contact and trusting a male who may be using manipulative pledges of love and care only to get her to have sex."[7]

Men have a powerful little chemical called *vasopressin*. This is our chemical cement, which causes married men to bond with their wives but does actual physical damage to the male brain when sex happens casually with a nonspouse. It's been nicknamed the "monogamy molecule" because it causes the man to feel attachment to a woman during physical intimacy.

In both females and males, the more casual sex you have without the stability of love and trust in marriage, the more destructive the habit becomes. Regardless of the *type* of activity—intercourse, oral sex, pornography, experimentation—casual sex actually damages the brain and its ability to function properly, especially for men. "The pattern of changing sex partners therefore seems to damage the ability to bond in a committed relationship. The inability to bond after multiple liaisons is almost like tape that loses its stickiness after being applied and removed multiple times."[8]

A Life of Consequences . . . or Rewards

We can't outsmart God. If we break His laws and abuse the bodies He gave us, we will suffer the consequences. You are not the exception to the rule. Our bodies are more than cells and atoms. They are intelligent and sensitive and must be treated with care. We can't live anywhere else but our own body, and we must live with them for the duration of our life on Earth. When we misuse our bodies in sexual relationships with other people (who also have bodies like ours), the effects will linger and remain in our bodies, in our hearts.

The facts prove that destructive sexual habits formed at a young age have disastrous consequences for years to follow, and it goes well beyond teen pregnancy and STDs. For one, "numerous studies show that when people have had sex before marriage, they are more likely to divorce when they do marry later on."[9] And five minutes on Google will show you thousands of reports from medical, psychological, government, and educational experts that all agree: divorce, though justified in cases of abuse, always negatively affects both spouses and all children involved. Having sex before you are mature enough to commit to marrying your partner may bring pleasure in the moment, but it brings pain in the future. But the consequences go beyond even the pain of divorce. One study showed that "individuals who have had sex before marriage are less likely to experience marital happiness. They are more likely to have difficulty adjusting to marriage and less likely to experience happiness, satisfaction, and love."[10]

Another result of sex, obviously, is pregnancy. God designed it to work like that, so even if you think protection will keep you from getting pregnant, the facts tell a different story.

- 20 percent of girls using birth control pills get pregnant within six months of having sex.
- 1 out of 5 teen couples using condoms get pregnant within a year.

- Half of all teen girls using any kind of contraception get pregnant within a year of having sex.
- 80 percent of unmarried teenage fathers never marry the mother of their baby.
- 80 percent of unmarried teenage moms eventually go on welfare to survive.
- 70 percent of unmarried moms never receive any financial support of any kind from the fathers of their babies.[11]

We cannot deny the fact that sex involves human bodies with brains, minds, feelings, and emotions. You can't have sex with someone and simply walk away. The effect is lasting, good or bad, for both parties. The facts don't lie. Consider that today in America, more than seventy million people have a sexually transmitted disease. (That's about one in five people.) Every year there are approximately nineteen million new cases. Of those new cases—contracted every year—half of them are people under the age of twenty-five.[12] Sex outside the context of marriage leads to a whole list of bad things: depression, anxiety, divorce, loneliness, regret, unhappiness, disease, unwanted pregnancy, poverty, and financial difficulty.

Sex itself is not to blame because sex is a good gift given to us by God for our pleasure and our flourishing. But when people try to violate the way God made our bodies and our brains, having careless sex outside of the safety of a covenant marriage, we pay a price. **God knows what's best for us. He designed our bodies and our souls. He understands how they function and how they should be used and protected. He's provided instruction through His Word. He's given us common sense. He's also given us the science that supports what He has told us in Scripture.** God has made provision for us. It begins by understanding His intent and design for sexuality and the human body.

God's Provision

God loves His children, and He would never give us rules and laws unless they were for our own benefit and blessing. And He hasn't left us on our own to try to figure it out. He instructs us in His Word, "Marriage must be respected by all, and the marriage bed kept undefiled, because God will judge immoral people and adulterers" (Hebrews 13:4).

That's as straightforward as you get. Marriage is the God-ordained institution within which sex should be celebrated. It provides stability, trust, safety, communication, and covenant. It should be respected, not tossed aside and ignored. The "marriage bed" is obviously referring to sex within a marriage. Paul the apostle instructs us to keep that marriage bed undefiled (pure, clean) because marriage is the proper context for things that happen "in the marriage bed." On the other hand, when sex is practiced outside of the context of marriage, those involved have no safety net of trust and care and communication, and the consequences will begin to pile up eventually.

God has established an order to His creation where sexual sin—all sex outside of marriage—leads to God's judgment. God takes sex seriously because sex deeply affects the children He dearly loves.

God values us and wants to protect us. You should do the same.

Protect your sexuality.

Protect your heart.

True Talk

1. Do you or someone you know have a heart problem? How do you know? What are some symptoms?

2. As a cure for heart problems, write a prescription using some of the Scriptures in this chapter. Focus on that Scripture, apply it to your life, until the symptoms subside.

3. Have you seen the effects of sexual sin around you? In what ways?

4. How can you begin today to help cure those around you of heart problems and their long-lasting effects?

CHAPTER 5

Purity from Within
—from Sharie

My little children, I am writing you these things so that you may not sin. But if anyone does sin, we have an advocate with the Father—Jesus Christ the Righteous One.

—1 John 2:1

The challenge in working on a project like this is finding the best way to warn you about the consequences of sex outside of marriage, *while* teaching you what a good gift sex really is, *while* assuring you that sexual sin can be forgiven without disqualifying you from God's best for your life, *while* not creating a chart where sexual sin is way worse than all others and irreversibly ruins your life.

We certainly don't want you to feel like damaged goods. It would be a tragedy for you to participate in the *True Love Project* and walk away feeling defeated and hopeless because you're not a virgin or because you messed up. I want to assure you that God can cleanse you, heal you, and forgive you.

No sin intimidates God. God's grace is greater than your past mistakes. Losing your virginity doesn't disqualify you from joy, peace, pleasure, or love. Jesus can take your biggest mess and make it your greatest message.

Just because you messed up, doesn't mean you give up.

Of course, you can't go back in time and unsin. None of us can rewind our lives and redo the things we regret. But because of God's love for you, He can redeem you from the guilt and shame you carry around, and He can restore your mind and body to be used for His glory. You may feel dirty, but Jesus makes you clean. You may have given up hope that you'll ever find true love, but God restores hope because His love is true and perfect and unconditional.

Gary Thomas, who has written extensively about sex, marriage, and relationships, says most people arrive on their wedding day with at least a decade's worth of sexual broken-ness from past relationships, pornography, abuse, and careless "fun" before they began life as a disciple of Christ. So please take courage that you are most certainly not alone in your quest for forgiveness and hope. In God's story He makes a way for us all to start over, to be made new, and to begin again.

In 1 John 2:1, John says he is writing a letter to his friends encouraging them not to sin. But of course he knows they will sin, so he wants to comfort them with a simple promise that Jesus Himself will be their advocate when they do sin. He will fight for them, He will defend them, and He will be righteous and holy for them when they cannot be righteous and holy on their own. This is our promise and our hope! Jesus is there for us when we take a detour from the right path, and He will not abandon us when we lose our way.

The first step on a long journey toward hope and healing from past mistakes is a simple little word—*forgiveness.*

It's easy to say. It's harder to give it and receive it.

Two Kinds of Forgiveness

You may need to receive God's forgiveness for the mistakes you've made.

You may need to forgive someone for the sins they have committed against you.

Regardless of which of these you need to wrestle with—and maybe it's both—forgiveness begins by looking to Jesus and being amazed at how much He forgave when He gave His life on the cross. The only way we can ever forgive another person or accept God's forgiveness of us is because of Jesus and through Jesus. To paraphrase the words of John the apostle, it would be awesome if you didn't sin. But when you do (and you will), you have someone who is there for you and will get your back. It's Jesus, and He will give you His righteousness in exchange for your sin.

> Forgiveness works the miracle of change.—Wilfred A. Peterson, *The Art of Living Treasure Chest*[1]

Receiving God's Forgiveness

Every time we experience hurt and disappointment in a relationship, we have a choice of what to do with our wrecked heart. We can receive forgiveness and take time to heal, or we can avoid the issue and hope it will go away. But refusing to deal with our failure and shame is like piling up garbage in a salvage dump and hoping it never begins to smell. Inevitably people notice when it begins to stink.

So if we refuse to be forgiven by Jesus, we will not be the only ones to smell our trash. It will invade the lives of those closest to us. We have to learn to forgive for our personal well-being and for the sake of our relationships with others.

Clayton and I have had countless conversations over the years with people of all ages who want to be forgiven and cleansed from their past, but they don't know how. They don't even know the first step. They're afraid they've messed things up so badly they'll never get married, enjoy sex, or live up to God's standard.

We always tell them, "You can't out sin God's grace." Then we share this verse with them: "If we confess our sins, He is faithful and righteous to forgive us our sins and to cleanse us from all unrighteousness" (1 John 1:9).

God doesn't hold your sin over your head. He doesn't throw it up in your face. He is tender and kind and graciously gives you another chance. And another one. And another one. The first step to this kind of new beginning is to confess your sin and repent of your sin.

Confess. Have you ever heard an old-timer use the phrase "fess up"? It means to admit to what you've done. The word *fess* means "to say or admit," and the word *con* simply means "with or alongside." So to confess something means to "say with or to agree with." When we confess our sin to God, we are fessing up, admitting to, and agreeing with God that we are imperfect and sinful. It means we aren't trying to hide our mistakes; we are bringing them out into the open before God.

Repent. To repent means to "turn away and turn around." When I sin and sense God's loving conviction, I choose to turn away from that sin and turn toward Jesus. I admit the action or the thought was wrong within itself, and I receive God's pardon and love. But don't think you can do this once and everything will be fine. I have to keep on repenting, all the time, every day. I will never stop sinning in this life, so I will never stop repenting either. His grace forgives me every time I come to Him in humility.

My Story of Abuse and Redemption

I was three years old when my mom and dad divorced. I didn't carry any memories of living with my dad with me after the divorce because I was so young. So I didn't know what to expect when my mom gave her heart to a new man three years later. Outwardly he seemed like a dream. He was from a good family, was financially stable, and liked to have a good time with my mom. But beneath the smiling face was a dark heart luring him into a perverted relationship with a young girl about six years old.

That young girl was me.

From the ages of six to ten, four and a half years of my life, this man acted on his polluted desires. He invaded my body and abused my heart. The fact that I had no correct under-standing of fatherly behavior and no relationship with my real dad blinded me to the fact that this man was a predator.

He was always around but never engaging. He would come to a dance recital here and there but never asked things like, "How was your day at school?" or "Did you enjoy your soccer game?" He wouldn't take my brother and me outside to kick the soccer ball, but he was more than willing to take me from my room in the mornings into his bed. He was only interested in me when he had me to himself under the covers, telling me where to lie and what to do behind closed doors. It all began with cuddling, but it progressed over the years. Eventually two events made me see how inappropriately he was treating me.

First, as a preteen I began to notice boys, and I began to like them. The sexual part of me began to come alive. Second, one Saturday morning my brother and I accidentally walked in on my mom and stepdad in their bedroom. I saw him doing things with my mom that he made me do with him.

The shame was instant and unbearable. I had to keep everything hidden at all costs. I was terrified that the person I loved the most in this world, my mom, would feel betrayed by me if she knew what he made me do. I was afraid she would hate me.

I was a terrified fifth-grader. I never invited friends over to my house because of my secret. I had to keep everyone at a distance. I felt different, dirty, and alone. I had friends, but I never let anyone too close. If they found out, where else could I ever go to be accepted or loved? If they came too close, would they become his victim too? Would he come after them? I would keep it all hidden and figure out a way to make it stop. Then God entered my story.

For some reason my mom regained an interest in church during this time. Sunday mornings were always tense as my mom and stepfather fought over whether we would go to the lake or to church. Often my mom's determination won out, and I was exposed to church, God's people, and the Bible; and I began to believe the amazing stories I heard in Sunday school. One of those stories changed my life.

My stepfather became bolder with his abuse. He stopped coming into my room to get me in the mornings but made me come to him. If I didn't, he'd hover over my bed until I complied. Then I decided I wasn't going to walk across the hall anymore to his bedroom. As I predicted, he wasn't going to let me off the hook. One morning he came to my room and began shaking me aggressively to wake me up. There is no way he thought I was still sleeping, but I refused to take my face out of my pillow. I wasn't sure what would happen next, but in that moment I remembered a picture of Jesus I had seen on the wall at church when I was younger. Seeing His face, I cried in my head for God to rescue me like He rescued the Israelites when He parted the Red Sea.

My body felt terrified, hot, and sweaty. But I noticed he stopped shaking me. So I peeked out from my pillow and saw him leaving. My temperature went down, and I lay there feeling cool air from my ceiling fan blow over my body. I had been rescued.

The next morning the same thing happened again. He came in, tried to get me to come with him, but I buried my head in the pillow and prayed to God. This time he left and never came back. Perhaps he was afraid of getting caught.

Perhaps the Lord heightened this fear to keep him from me. He had a lot to lose with a successful career in computer engineering, lakefront property, a nice sports car, and a spotless reputation. I don't know why he stopped, but I do know that God answered the prayers of a little girl who hadn't yet received Jesus as Savior but already knew that God was a Saver.

With a past like mine, I wondered if I had anything beautiful to offer my husband. Would the man of my future see me as dirty, tainted, and used? Or could he see past my abuse to find the jewel God had rescued?

Maybe the shadow of your past did not originate with someone else, but it was your own doing. You said yes to a boyfriend before you were ready. Or maybe your physical desires seemed uncontrollable, and you convinced your girlfriend to give in. Maybe you didn't go "all the way," but you know what you did was too much, too soon, and too fast. Maybe your shame is hidden in your mind's fantasy. You haven't been with anyone, but the visions in your head torment you.

Sexual sin is paralyzing and embarrassing. We want to hide or escape. But God is not paralyzed or embarrassed by our sin. Sin doesn't intimidate God because He conquered it. He knows the cure. He knows that "forgiving is the only way to get ourselves free from the trap of persistent and unfair pain. Far from being a dishonest denial of reality, forgiving is not even possible unless we own the painful truth of what happened to us."[2]

He wants us forgive our offenders for sins committed against us. He also wants us to forgive ourselves for the sins we've committed with our own bodies against ourselves and against others.

I've had to learn how to do both. And by God's grace I am still learning.

Extending Forgiveness to Others

My story of abuse brought me face-to-face with both realities. First, I had to receive God's forgiveness even though I had committed no sin. Through the sin of my stepfather, God made me aware of what sin is and that I too was a sinner in need of His forgiveness. Second, I had to choose to forgive the man who victimized me for almost five years. I could only extend that kind of forgiveness because Jesus had extended it to me.

Here are a few things to keep in mind when you're trying to forgive.

1. Forgiveness is specific. Forgiveness can't be vague, or it will be ineffective. It needs to be specific to the person, the event, or the action that causes the pain. So when you are searching your heart and know that something is wrong, look for a *who* and a *what*. Who hurt you? Whom did you hurt?

What happened? Why did that cause such grief or shame? Don't settle for generic answers. Get specific.

Here are some steps to help you forgive specifically:

- **Think.** Come to as much clarity as you can on what actually happened. Focusing on painful things from your past takes time and effort, but you can face them with God's grace.
- **Evaluate.** Ask important questions about the offense. Was there intent to harm? Was it an accident? a misunderstanding? Did the person know what he or she was doing? Was it a lapse in judgment?
- **Talk.** Consult with a friend or counselor. Speak with your pastor. Externalize your emotions by journaling. If possible, apologize to anyone you may have hurt. Get the help all of us need after we have been damaged.
- **Feel.** Take time to be alone with yourself, without the distractions of TV or your phone. Get in touch with what you feel. Feelings are sloppy things, and you may need time to put a name on what's going on inside of you when you face the hurt head-on.
- **Pray.** Talk to God honestly. He knows all the details of the sin, and He still loves you, so don't hold anything back.

"Forgiving is a tough act to perform when bad things are done to us. Here is a chance to be honest with God. Tell him how much it hurts, how full of hate you are. Admit you need help, ask for it, and use it when it comes."—Lewis B. Smedes, *The Art of Forgiving*[3]

Specific forgiveness can be scary. It's uncomfortable and messy. It's easier not to worry about the details and throw a big "forgiveness blanket" over the situation, hoping it will go away. This is a coping mechanism that provides no cure. When we make forgiveness undetermined, indefinite, and unclear, we take away its power because we don't truly release our offenses. Vague forgiveness works no true healing in our lives; it only pauses it. We understand this when we look to the author of forgiveness Himself.

2. Forgiveness is how God heals us. God's first act of forgiveness was in the garden of Eden. When Adam and Eve disobeyed God's clear command, He had every right to turn them into dust the moment they rebelled. But instead of vengeance, God chose to forgive. In this way, "God is the original, master forgiver. I am not at all sure that any of us would have had the imagination enough to see the possibilities in this way to heal the wrongs of this life had he not done it first."[4]

When creating the world, "God said, 'Let there be light,' and there was light. God saw that the light was good, and God separated the light from the darkness" (Genesis 1:3–4). God takes the dark, sinful things and makes light shine into them. At the beginning of time, there was only darkness before He put light into it. He saw the tragedy of Adam and Eve's decision, and He made a plan of redemption. He uses this same process for the darkness in our hearts. When we confess our sins and repent of them, He begins to shine the light of Christ in our hearts. This light shows us what hides in the darkness. His light convicts us, but it doesn't condemn us.

Second Corinthians 4:6 reminds us, "For God who said, 'Let light shine out of darkness,' has shone in our hearts to give the light of the knowledge of God's glory in the face of Jesus Christ." God shows us our sin so we can repent and be healed. God doesn't show it to us to shame us but rather to change us. Looking back at where we've failed is not easy. But when He shines His light on hurting places, specific areas, painful memories, and deep regrets, we can see the "face of Jesus Christ" and look to Him as our source of forgiveness and love.

When God shined His light on the abuse I suffered during childhood, I saw the tragedy, but I also saw the hope. I've forgiven a lot, but even today God may show me a place of darkness. I have a choice of whether to cover it back up or take that road toward restoration.

Your life may not be void of pain, but it is also not void of possibility. God wants to turn our hopelessness into redemption and turn feelings of condemnation into deliverance.

3. Forgiveness is how we heal ourselves. When I was in college, my boyfriend of two years broke up with me on a mission trip. A mission trip! Talk about awkward! I tried to avoid him, but the group was always together. I refused to show my inner turmoil in public, but the minute I got back to my room, my best friend absorbed my anguish and anger. The first month of the trip, I resented his smiles, his presence, and even his prayers. How could a guy like that have a heart, right?

I don't know how you can be so angry at someone and yet want them back, but I did. I determined to keep it together. I was going to show him what a great girl he had lost. (I am not condoning this attitude, only being transparent. This is not a testimony but a confession.)

A month passed, and we were still on the mission trip together. I knew we would be home in a couple of weeks, and I was beginning to get over him. But then he approached me and asked if I'd take him back. Talk about a heartbreaker! I didn't trust him or my own feelings, so I made him talk about his intentions with my campus minister. After their meeting the three of us sat down for a big talk.

Apparently the minute my boyfriend arrived overseas, he struggled with how to concentrate on God while being in a relationship during a mission trip. He apologized for wrecking my heart, and he repented for how he'd handled everything. I thought about it for a few days, and then I took him back. We had a month of bliss ministering together in Poland. My campus minister assured me that my boyfriend intended to pursue marriage when we came back to the United States.

We arrived back on campus, and the semester started fine until he showed up at my apartment one night. After an hour of awkward conversation, he said he needed to "sacrifice me as Abraham sacrificed Isaac." If God brought me back to him, then it was meant to be, but if not, he would have his answer. That's how he broke my heart the second time.

After a double-dump, I have to say I never looked his way again. He broke my heart in a way that no one else had ever hurt me. I had feelings and dreams of revenge and pain for him. But eventually the unforgiveness began to eat at my soul. Holding onto this offense was making me bitter. I couldn't stand myself for being so gullible. I was mad at my friends for being nice to him. My joy and contentment were replaced by anger and hostility.

When people hurt us, we want them to suffer. We want them to hurt as we have hurt and to the same degree (or more!). Sure, this is a natural human reaction, but it's also emotionally self-destructive. Lewis Smedes explains: "Hate is the most self-righteous of all emotions. We feel deliriously righteous when we hate the evil creature who viciously assaulted us. No one ever feels the pleasure of self-righteousness with such lip-smacking satisfaction as a person chewing on his own hate. This is why we love our hate, cuddle it, feed it, stroke it, and above all justify it. But let it settle in for a while, take over the best room in our souls, and it becomes a disagreeable guest who will not leave when our party is over."[5]

Whether passive or aggressive, our hurt leaves us calling out to God to make bad things happen to the bad person who did bad things to us. That is what hate is. When we begin to forgive, however, we reverse that destructive process. It may take a little while before you are ready to forgive, but don't give up. Your goal is to let go of your anger and hate for your sake, for their sake, and for God's sake.

God is not asking you to work the miracle of forgiveness, but He is asking you to be an active participant in the health of your mind, soul, and spirit. A redeemed soul still requires maintenance. As we're told in Philippians, a Christian still needs to work on his relationship with God, knowing that God is the one who empowers you to want good things and do good things. "So then, my dear friends, just as you have always obeyed, not only in my presence, but now even more in my absence, work out your own salvation with fear and trembling. For it is God who is working in you, enabling you both to desire and to work out His good purpose" (Philippians 2:12–13).

When I was in high school, I read a story that illustrates this point perfectly. A pastor from a small village in a poor country stood in front of a table of believers breaking bread for Communion when a man walked into the back of the room. The pastor saw him and froze. He was unable to breathe or speak. The church members were unsure of how to react. He eventually resumed serving Communion. The pastor told a friend after Communion that the man who had entered the church was the very same man who had brutally murdered his father years earlier. The murderer had become a Christian and was there to take Communion. The pastor realized as he served this man that he had to forgive the man who killed his father. They had both been cleansed by the blood of Christ. The murderer was already forgiven by Jesus. The pastor had to follow His example.

Forgiveness is not easy. God's forgiveness cost Him His Son. The gift of forgiveness cost Jesus blood, sweat, tears, torture, betrayal, ridicule, and wrath. So stop feeling guilty or discouraged when forgiveness proves hard. You are not alone. Sometimes, as I've let go of my offenses, I could feel the hatred and bitterness dying inside of me. I can't imagine what that village pastor felt inside as he forgave his father's murderer. When we feel that freedom, we can fellowship with Christ.

4. Forgiveness is a gift, not an obligation. My mom ended up divorcing the man who sexually abused me, but then she remarried a man when I was a teenager. He was not kind to me emotionally. He crossed the line when he complimented me physically, and when I told him it was inappropriate, he said I could not receive a compliment because of my abusive background. He demanded that I call him "Dad." This created division between my biological father and me, but it was beyond my control.

As a Christian, I wanted to honor my parents, but I felt exasperated and confused. Which parent should I honor? When I asked advice from church members, I got, "You just need to forgive because Jesus forgave . . . seventy times seven." As a young and growing follower of Christ, I would choose to forgive my stepdad, and I assumed that because my heart had changed, his had also. But it never did.

I began to resent and even question the theology of forgiveness. It didn't feel like it was working. I felt forced into forgiveness.

But forgiveness is a gift, not an obligation. Do you know anyone who has genuinely forgiven out of obligation? My husband and I have often noticed that people who are caught in their sin rarely experience true repentance and life change. They may say they are sorry when caught, but often they don't change their behavior because their hearts have not experienced true conviction. The concept is the same with forgiveness. Not even God forgave out of mandate. God forgives because something within His being is bent on seeing us redeemed rather than condemned. This should be our motivation as well.

Forgiveness must originate from a personal change of heart: a desire to give something undeserved, trusting this will help heal you. Lewis Smedes describes the process, "Forgiving is a gift, not a duty. It is meant to heal, not to obligate. Use the gift as often as it takes to set you free from a miserable past you cannot shake."[6] This doesn't mean it always feels good. It may be hard to do, and you may have to give your hurt to God over and over, but the choice to forgive is willful and not coerced.

This is where the concept of "seventy times seven" comes in. In Genesis 4:23–24, a man named Lamech killed a man who wounded him. He confessed to his wives what he had done, but instead of repentance he declared himself justified. He claimed he had the right to take vengeance seventy-seven times for how he was treated.

Fast-forward to the New Testament where Peter asks Jesus how many times he should have to forgive a brother who sins against him. "Up to seven times?" Peter asked, undoubtedly thinking that answer was admirable. But Jesus trumps it with His answer: "I tell you, not as many as seven, . . . but 70 times seven" (Matthew 18:21–22).

I know I've asked myself how many times I have to keep forgiving the people who wronged me. How many times do I have to let people off the hook? If we were to take this verse literally, I suppose we could stop at 490. But I don't think this verse is about the number. Jesus is explaining to Peter that there is no magic number because we live in a world where we're never completely sheltered from sinful desires and influences. Therefore, we always have to be prepared to give and receive forgiveness.

5. Forgiveness doesn't always bring restoration. Finally, we must know that giving or receiving forgiveness is not a guarantee that the relationship can (or should) be restored. I lived in a dilemma with my second stepfather for years. When I was around him, the only way I knew to survive his manipulation was to put up emotional barriers because my heart was afraid of his criticism and control.

However, when I left for college and had time away, I would start to open up and feel free. I developed friendships with people who did not tear me down to make themselves feel important. In these times I realized how hard and calloused I was when I was back home around him. I wondered if the conflict in our relationship was my fault. It only took two trips back home (and two downward emotional spirals resulting from his harsh words to me) to understand that the barriers I had created were actually healthy and necessary for my emotional survival.

Even though I felt Jesus change me inside, my stepfather remained hard-hearted and stubborn. His heart toward me was no different, regardless of what the Holy Spirit was doing in me. Even though I was willing to let go of my offenses, this did not mean he would treat me any differently. My outlook around him changed when I realized that he was my "seventy times seven" person. I had to be willing to keep forgiving him even though he never changed. I knew we would never have a restored relationship. But I chose to forgive as a holy habit.

In these cases we are always responsible to forgive for the benefit of our souls, but we are not responsible for how the person we forgive reacts. Smedes explains: "When we

> Forgiveness is not an occasional act; it is a constant attitude.—Martin Luther King Jr.

forgive we see the person who wounded us as a fellow human being worthy of our love, and in that sense we reconcile ourselves to him. But being reconciled to him as a human being and embracing him as a partner are two different things, and we should keep them apart. Whether we heal the relationship depends pretty much on the forgiven person."[7]

We are also completely justified in setting boundaries to keep ourselves from exploitation and abuse. The same principle applies when you're struggling to believe you are forgiven for your mistakes. When you finally receive God's forgiveness, the last thing you want to do is attempt to restore a sinful relationship. Some relationships are bad. Period. Run away from them, and don't look back.

The Fruits of Forgiveness

There are also beautiful stories of people who have restored relationships because they were able to see each other's humanity, forgive, and reconcile.

I have a friend who wanted to be a virgin when she married. After a few bad decisions based on insecurity, she lost all hope of that dream. She gave in to her boyfriend and then, because she felt she couldn't go back and be pure again, started sleeping around in college. After a season of discouragement and guilt, she found the courage to tell her parents. She was afraid of their reaction, but they embraced her and loved her as they wept together as a family.

They also came up with a plan: they decided to move forward together. Their church was participating in the True Love Waits campaign, and she decided this was the perfect opportunity for her to embrace fully the forgiveness and grace of God. Her sister walked forward to make her commitment to save all sexual intimacy for marriage. Then my friend, who had believed the lie that she was used and dirty, took her dad's hand, and together they recommitted to finish strong, to walk in God's grace, and to look forward to a life of service to God and, eventually, a Christ-centered marriage. This is a true and hope-filled story of a reconciled relationship rebuilt from an act of forgiveness. My friend was reconciled to her parents, reconciled to God, and reconciled to herself. She no longer hated who she had become because she embraced herself as God saw her: forgiven, redeemed, whole, and beloved!

I was sitting in the audience when my pastor Perry Noble asked, "Why is it that we know God *sees* us when we sin, but we are not sure He *hears* when we ask forgiveness?" I've felt this question many times as I pray. "God, I've asked You a million times to forgive me. Do You hear me this time? Will You forgive me again?"

> Yahweh, if You considered sins, Lord, who could stand? But with You there is forgiveness, so that You may be revered.
> —Psalm 130:3-4

His answer is always the same: He loves you, and He has already forgiven you through His Son, Jesus Christ. Rest in His mercy, not your ability. Receive the gift of forgiveness He freely offers you. And extend forgiveness to others with that same generosity. Keep confessing and keep repenting and keep receiving and keep forgiving.

Make His forgiveness part of your story because, after all, it's a part of His.

True Talk

1. As you read through this chapter on forgiveness, into what areas of darkness in your life did God shed light?

2. What do you need to be forgiven for?

3. And whom do you need to forgive?

4. Spend some quiet time with God right now, soaking in His forgiveness and extending that same grace to those who have wronged you. Allow that forgiveness quietly to change your heart and your life.

CHAPTER 6

Direction and Destination

How happy is everyone who fears the LORD, who walks in His ways!

—Psalm 128:1

Everyone ends up somewhere, but few people end up somewhere on purpose.

—Craig Groeschel

Soon after I graduated from college, some friends from another state decided they were going to come visit me and my roommates while they were on a road trip. Our house of young, single guys was always open to buddies that needed a place to crash for the night or just drop in. We were excited to have guests. We were going to eat pizza and watch sports and stay up late. I specifically told them how to get to our house. Because I traveled for a living as an evangelist and speaker, I was meticulous about directions. My livelihood depended on having clear directions to my destination.

I told them, "When you get near Spartanburg on I-26, begin looking for signs for I-85. Take I-85 North until you see signs for Highway 150. Take that exit into Boiling Springs." They said they would be at our house about three o'clock.

We kept waiting and waiting. They never showed up. Several hours after they said they would arrive, they called me from a gas station just north of Atlanta.

"Clayton, you live in North Carolina, right? For some reason we are in Georgia. We did exactly what you said. We drove up from Columbia, South Carolina, to Spartanburg and then we got on I-85. We did what you said, but we're nowhere near your house."

It took me less than a nanosecond to realize what they had done. They were on the right interstate, but they were in the wrong state. They were on the right road, but they were going the wrong direction. I told them to go north. They went south.

It was the right road but the wrong direction.

And the wrong direction always leads to the wrong destination.

They really wanted to come to my house, but while heading the wrong way, no matter how far they drove or how frustrated they became, the only way they were ever going to arrive at their desired destination was to change directions. They needed to turn around.

Sexual desire is the right road, but you must steer that desire in the right direction if you intend to arrive at the correct destination. Sexual desire is hardwired into you, and it is a sign of something greater than sex. It's a reflection of the need for lasting love found in friendships and marriage and ultimately in an eternal relationship with your Lord and Redeemer, Jesus Christ.

Andy Stanley says that direction, not intention, determines the destination. This seems like a pretty obvious rule, but so few people seem to follow it. Yet if you want to enjoy the blessing of true love, the contentment of being single and satisfied in the family of God, and eventually the joy of a lifelong relationship with a spouse who loves Christ and makes you a better person, you will need to apply this wisdom.

And you need to begin now.

Yes, you may need to turn around and change direction. And you may actually need to decide where you want to wind up because you're going to end up somewhere eventually.

Why not go there intentionally?

Your intention doesn't get you to your destination. But your intention can prompt you to take action by heading in the right direction. If your intention is to protect your heart so you can eventually find true love, enter into a covenant marriage, and grow old with your mate, you will have to back that intention up with some action. It starts by heading in the right direction.

What's the Goal?

Before you can strike out in the right direction, you must decide where you want to go. Without that crucial piece of information being settled at the outset, you're wasting time and energy going nowhere. Think about what the psalmist is saying when he writes these words: "Your word is a lamp for my feet and a light on my path. I have solemnly sworn to keep Your righteous judgments" (Psalm 119:105–106).

His life is a path, but he cannot see where he's going or what may lie along the path to trip him up on his way. He is on the right road, but to make sure he is heading in the right direction, he has chosen to light the way with God's Word. He solemnly swears to live by Scripture, to submit himself to God and His ways, and to allow God's wisdom to illuminate the dark, exposing any trap or temptation that could hurt him. He believes God's Word is his only hope for arriving at his destination.

He goes on to say, "My life is constantly in danger, yet I do not forget Your instruction. The wicked have set a trap for me, but I have not wandered from Your precepts. I have Your decrees as a heritage forever; indeed, they are the joy of my heart. I am resolved to obey Your statutes to the very end" (Psalm 119:109–112).

The method he uses to stay focused on the right direction is simple: he remembers God's instructions. He remembers God's precepts. He remembers God's decrees. He celebrates them! They give him joy! He makes a serious commitment to obey God saying, "I am resolved to obey your statutes to the very end"—the destination. He knows where he wants to go, and he knows the only way to get there is to fix his eyes and his heart on God and His Word. You'll find no better chunk of Scripture than this one to help guide you toward Jesus and a life He can use for His glory.

What's your ultimate destination? Is your goal to have really great sex one day? Are you living for the wedding day? Do you only dream about the wedding dress or the honeymoon night? Although there's certainly no harm in imagining those special moments, they should never be the primary motivation for marrying another person. Marriage, though godly and good and wonderful, is not eternal. If you idolize marriage and make it your sole pursuit in life, you will work for and worship the myth of a "perfect marriage" or a "perfect mate" and be crushed when you discover neither one of these exists. You will never have a perfect marriage. There is no "perfect sex." And there are certainly no perfect spouses. **As a matter of fact, when you meet the person you want to marry,**

remember that this person was so sinful, Jesus had to die on the cross to save him or her.

Look around, and you will see people chasing all sorts of dreams. Success. Financial security. Living debt-free. A college scholarship. The honor roll. A skinny body. A bigger house. Getting elected. Becoming valedictorian or team captain.

What's your primary pursuit? Have you ever asked yourself what your life's goal is? Have you ever even thought about it?

What is your "big win" in life?

I want you to think about it. I want you to settle it right here and right now if you haven't already made your decision. But before you do, I want to speak with you openly. Allow me to help you consider what you want to gain, specifically in the area of love and relationships.

A Dose of Reality

Craving a physical and emotional connection with another person is completely natural. It's how God wired our minds and bodies. It's normal to desire intimacy and sexual pleasure. It's how God designed the human race to self-perpetuate and survive. It's altogether good to dream about getting married and sharing your life with another person. It was God's created order going all the way back to Eden in Genesis.

Although the deep desire for these things is healthy and good, there's also a serious danger in subconsciously making love or sex or marriage the ultimate goal of your life because, if having great sex or an awesome marriage becomes your primary pursuit, you are setting yourself up for disappointment.

You could be heading in the wrong direction because you're aiming at the wrong destination.

What if your marriage turns out to be way harder than you expected? What if that perfect guy you dated turns out to be a stubborn sinner once you marry him? What if that gorgeous college girl you fell for fifteen years ago has three of your children and gains forty pounds? What if the sex on your honeymoon is awkward and uncomfortable? What if, a couple years into your marriage, you barely have sex once a week? What if the abuse you suffered or the mistakes you made in the past make it nearly impossible for you to desire sex with your husband or wife?

Or . . . what if you remain a virgin until you're married hoping that sex will be the most earth-shattering, mind-bending joy you've ever known . . . and it's not?

I guarantee you that one or some of these will happen to you at some point after you're married. You will realize that you married a sinner. Your spouse will let you down. You will disappoint your spouse repeatedly. You will realize that sex is a by-product of trust, communication, and friendship and that those take time and effort. Your children and your job will make finding time for each other more difficult, in turn making it more difficult to enjoy sex. Life will include frustration and hurt and insecurity. And sex will not fix it, even if you are a virgin when you get married.

Am I saying you shouldn't pursue virginity? Absolutely not. If you are a virgin, you are blessed. With accurate expectations the road will be so much easier. You can avoid many of the regrets and the baggage others experience when they don't wait. My wife and I were both virgins when we got married, by the grace of God, and we rejoice that we waited until our honeymoon night to have intercourse. So yes, you should without a doubt pursue virginity. But virginity must not be the primary goal of your life, even though it's a good and godly thing to pursue.

The goal is not just to be a virgin on your wedding day. The goal is to be found faithful on judgment day.

Virginity shouldn't be your ultimate destination, though it's a godly goal. Marriage is a wonderful gift of God, but it can't be your "big win" in life. Sex, though satisfying and fun, is too small a thing to spend your entire life chasing. The one and only thing worthy of your entire life, of becoming your ultimate goal, is to know Jesus and one day have Him welcome you into His eternal kingdom.

So as you pick your destination, realize that Jesus is better than a good marriage, great sex, or even being able to say you were a virgin on your honeymoon. You could have the picture-perfect marriage . . . or the most awesome sex . . . or be a virgin as you walk down the aisle on your wedding day. But if you didn't have Jesus, none of those would satisfy you. None of those would save you.

What's my point? It's simple.

Jesus is the destination.

He is the "big win." He is the goal. He is the finish line. He is the treasure at the end of life. If you get all the other things you always wanted—romance, family, vacations, big house, lots of money, lots of sex—but you don't get Jesus, you gain nothing in the end.

Jesus knew that this would happen to people, so He warned us of arriving at the wrong destination, predicting that many would show up on judgment day empty-handed with nothing to show for their lives. Consider these words straight from the mouth of Jesus Christ: "For whoever wants to save his life will lose it, but whoever loses his life because of Me and the gospel will save it. For what does it benefit a man to gain the whole world yet lose his life? What can a man give in exchange for his life? For whoever is ashamed of Me and of My words in this adulterous and sinful generation, the Son of Man will also be ashamed of him when He comes in the glory of His Father with the holy angels" (Mark 8:35–38).

This is perhaps the clearest warning Jesus ever gave about the direction people take with their desires. This is a warning about arriving at the wrong destination. This is a warning about final judgment. He is predicting that people will chase after all sorts of treasures that will never give them what they want. He goes so far as to say they will lose their lives in the process, and He alludes to their eternal separation from God on judgment day. This is the ultimate loss—to spend your life chasing after a big win and find yourself losing everything in the end.

In the Gospel of Matthew, Jesus gives a similar warning: "Not everyone who says to Me, 'Lord, Lord!' will enter the kingdom of heaven, but only the one who does the will of My Father in heaven. On that day many will say to Me, 'Lord, Lord, didn't we prophesy in Your name, drive out demons in Your name, and do many miracles in Your name?' Then I will announce to them, 'I never knew you! Depart from Me, you lawbreakers!'" (Matthew 7:21–23).

Talk about the ultimate shocker! That passage takes my breath away. Imagine spending your life living for one big thing and then being blindsided on judgment day when Jesus reveals that you were going the wrong direction the whole time. That's precisely what Jesus is warning us about. (And really, how can we be blindsided when He's already warned us about it?)

So, what is the ultimate destination you should choose? According to these verses it's Jesus and His gospel. The people in this passage had chosen wrong destinations even though the things they were running after were good. Don't you agree that preaching, casting out demons, and doing miracles in the name of Jesus are good things? Of course they are, but they are small things compared to Jesus Himself. When you turn something *good* into your *god*, it always ends badly. There is only one God, Jesus Christ, and no other "god" can satisfy or save you.

Pursuing sexual purity, virginity, true love, and a good marriage are wonderful things you should run after. But the only way you will accomplish these goals is to make Jesus your big win. The only way to arrive at these destinations is to make Jesus your ultimate destination.

Dr. Richard Ross, the author of the original *True Love Waits*, e-mailed me as I was working on this project. He said: "My purity is for His delight primarily. If I am still single at age seventy, my heart will be full of joy over the relationship I have shared with my regal King, thankful that immorality never harmed the depth of intimacy we have shared. As my King Regent, He has every right to all of me—including the sexual me. I am His alone. Marriage then becomes the icing on the cake, not the cake. He is the main thing, the only thing that matters ultimately. I am waiting to stand before my King on the new earth, waiting for His 'well done.' I am waiting for unimaginable closeness with Him forever. And I want nothing on earth that impinges on my delight in Him forever."

Choose your ultimate destination now. Only Jesus is big enough and good enough for you to commit your entire life to. Once you give yourself totally and completely to Him, you take action. As a child of God, you submit your relationships and your choices and your past mistakes to Christ. You know your destination, so you head in that direction.

Pick your destination.

Take action.

Head in the right direction.

Paul the apostle understood what it was like to have his ultimate desire changed. He went from hating Christianity to being its greatest evangelist. For Paul, Jesus was the prize. Read what he wrote in a letter to his beloved friends in the ancient city of Philippi: "Not that I have already reached the goal or am already fully mature, but I make every effort to take hold of it because I also have been taken hold of by Christ Jesus. Brothers, I do not consider myself to have taken hold of it. But one thing I do: Forgetting what is behind and reaching forward to what is ahead, I pursue as my goal the prize promised by God's heavenly call in Christ Jesus" (Philippians 3:12–14).

> "Will power is weak against the force of desire. If we wish to change what we do, we must change what we desire."—Wendy Farley, *The Wounding and Healing of Desire*[1]

Take Action

It's not enough to have good intentions when it comes to true love, a godly marriage, or lifelong faithfulness to Christ. You have to take action. So, how do you do that? Where do you start? Allow me to illustrate the necessity of taking action immediately in the area of your relationships, no matter how old you are or what stage of life you're in.

I'm a football kind of guy. I played for fourteen years. I love college football and the NFL. I watch as many games as possible. And even though this happened to me twenty-five years ago, it's still as fresh in my mind as if it happened this morning.

As a freshman I tried out for varsity football at Hillcrest High School. I was told I had virtually no shot at making the team at such a young age. Still I decided to go for it, and it paid off. I made the team and even started the first game of the season.

Among the many things our head coach taught us was the danger of "standing around on the field." During a play you had to keep moving. If you stopped, a player from the other team would see you standing still and interpret that as an invitation to knock your head off. If you weren't moving, you were a target. My coach yelled and screamed constantly about this. He warned us that we could get seriously hurt if we didn't keep moving down the field.

In my first game as a varsity football player, I experienced what my coach had warned me about. I snapped the ball to the quarterback, blocked the nose guard, and watched our running back get tackled a few yards down the field. As I stood still watching him go down, a guy from the other team came at me like a bullet. All I saw was a white streak to my left a split second before he hit me with the force of a comet. One moment I was standing there oblivious, and the next moment I saw Julie Andrews singing and twirling on the top of a mountain in Austria.

He knocked me out cold, all because I stopped moving.

My coach didn't have a crystal ball. He just had common sense and experience. I should have listened to him, but I had to learn the hard way. If you just stand around doing nothing, you will get blindsided.

That common sense is true for relationships too. The best way to guarantee a miserable life of breakups, regret, broken hearts, and divorce is to be passive and lazy and do nothing. If you don't take action and keep moving, you'll wind up flat on your back. You'll hop from one relationship to the next looking for someone to solve all your problems and make you happy. You'll be discouraged, angry, depressed, and resentful. You will be tempted to blame everyone else. Eventually you'll get numb to the pain and stop caring about true love. You'll settle for temporary affection, the hookup, the booty call, porn, or the one-night stand.

And one day you'll wake up and realize you're all alone. You'll take inventory of the years you wasted chasing the wrong thing. You'll look back at the road you've been on and realize you were heading in the wrong direction the whole time. At that point you can repent and turn around. You can submit to the lordship of Jesus Christ, and He can transform you by His grace. He can forgive you and you can start over.

You can do that. Or you can go another direction. You can take action right now by doing the small, simple things that are required to prepare you for your husband or wife, realizing that a good marriage is just part of arriving at your ultimate destination of knowing Jesus and belonging to Him.

The First Step

We know intuitively that we can't do this without help. God knows this better than we do, so He has given us His Word to guide and instruct us in our pursuit of holiness and purity and ultimately true love. I like to think of it like this:

Submission ➡ Direction ➡ Instruction ➡ Action ➡ Destination

Submission. Give up your rights as your own Lord and surrender total control of your relationships to God. Trust God fully with your future. Believe that He loves you and would never tell you to do something that was bad for you.

Remember that He doesn't want anything from you. He wants something for you!

Direction. Decide where you want to go, what kind of person you want to be, and what kind of marriage you want to have. Look down the road of your life and imagine a marriage that is built on a solid foundation—not fickle feelings but firm faith in Jesus. Dedicate yourself to moving toward that goal. Write it down in the margin of your Bible or your personal journal. And if God gives you the gift of remaining single, you will find joy and fulfillment in Jesus and His church, being uniquely positioned to focus more energy on ministry and kingdom work.

Instruction. Yield your mind and your heart to the wisdom of Scripture by reading it, meditating on it, and memorizing it. Ask an older Christian to mentor you. Submit to the authority of your pastor, your parents, and your spiritual leaders. Sit on the front row at church with a pen and a pad and take notes until your hand cramps. Fill your iPod with sermons that challenge you. Read books that instruct you in the ways of being a true disciple. Choose the voices you will listen to, and turn off the ones that don't encourage you to become more like Christ.

Action. Begin putting the wisdom of God into practice by doing what it says on a regular basis, applying it and obeying it as a holy habit. Set standards for the people you will date. Put a filter on your computer. Ask some friends to check up on you and hold you accountable. Meet weekly with a pastor or a mentor. End a bad relationship that's pulling you down. Cancel your cable if you have to. Avoid parties and social events where you will be tempted to hook up with an ex. Get serious about Jesus and your destiny!

Destination. Believe that following Jesus by faith and living under His lordship will ultimately bring you joy, peace, and His will for your relationships. Believe that, unless He's given you the gift of singleness, He will direct you to another godly person with whom you can share your life when the time is right. If you can trust Jesus to save you from hell, you can trust that you won't miss true love as long as you are chasing after Jesus and are submitted to His will as the Lord of your life.

I hope you don't think I'm trying to give you a cute little formula to follow because it's way more complex and involved than "five easy steps to a perfect life." With that said, the truth remains: there is a pattern and a rhythm to following Jesus as His disciple, and the Bible is filled with promises that if we remain faithful to God through obedience, He will fulfill His purpose in us.

That's not a quick fix. It's an eternal promise from the living God!

Consider how imperative His Word is when it comes to taking action and moving in the right direction. Psalm 119:9 helps to answer that with this: "How can a young man keep his way pure? By keeping Your word." That's just one simple verse! Do you see how practical and direct that is? If you want to keep yourself pure, you need to live according to God's instruction. This isn't brain surgery or rocket science. It's so simple that we often miss it.

Following the directions gets you to the destination!

That's just the beginning. Scripture is packed full of truth because it was written by God, and as we saw at the beginning, it's part of His bigger story of redeeming and restoring all that He made.

So, what do you do when you feel like the temptation to sin is just too strong? Does the Bible have instruction about that? Absolutely! Check out Psalm 119:11: "I have treasured Your word in my heart so that I may not sin against You."

Read that again.

The Bible says right there in plain English that when you choose to open your heart to the wisdom and direction of Scripture, it will displace sin. *It will actually keep you away from sin.* It will strengthen you, help you resist temptation, and continue to move you forward in the direction you want to go.

We've barely scratched the surface. There's more in Psalm 119:24: "Your decrees are my delight and my counselors."

How many people do you know who are addicted to relationship drama and are constantly dumping their drama on their friends (or on you), expecting everyone else to be their counselor? This verse says that God's Word can be your counselor. You can delight in God's statutes. Instead of staying up all night long, crying and depressed, spilling your guts like an emotional wreck to you friends, you can avoid that nonsense by applying the wisdom of the Bible to your relationships.

The Bible is probably a better counselor anyway. (I'm just saying.)

Following the directions gets you to the destination, but it starts with submission, yielding yourself to the wisdom of God in the Bible.

Can you say for yourself what the psalmist says in 119:14–16? "I rejoice in the way revealed by Your decrees as much as in all riches. I will meditate on Your precepts and think about Your ways. I will delight in Your statutes; I will not forget Your word." If not yet, that's OK! Just take the first step in the right direction, and you'll be on your way.

The Bible offers direction and instruction for every circumstance you'll ever find yourself in, whether it's lust, insecurity, fear, or selfishness. Just read these three verses and notice how supernaturally accurate God's Word is: "Direct me in the path of your commands, for there I find delight. Turn my heart toward your statutes and not toward selfish gain. Turn my eyes away from worthless things; preserve my life according to your word" (Psalm 119:35–37 NIV).

When you're confused about whom to date or marry, "Direct me in the path of your commands."

When your heart wants something you know you shouldn't pursue, "Turn my heart toward your statutes and not toward selfish gain."

When you're struggling with lust or tempted to look at porn, "Turn my eyes away from worthless things."

What about the times when you're really lonely and all your friends are dating, and you don't have anyone? Nobody calls you or texts you, it's been months since you had a date, and you don't even have any prospects? You begin to doubt this whole "submission-direction-instruction-action-destination" thing. You wonder if you can really trust God's Word because it's clearly not working.

Try this: "LORD, Your word is forever; it is firmly fixed in heaven. Your faithfulness is for all generations; You established the earth, and it stands firm" (Psalm 119:89–90).

When you doubt your decision to trust God's Word, "Your word is forever; it is firmly fixed in heaven."

When you wonder if He can be trusted to bring you the right mate, "Your faithfulness is for all generations."

When you're afraid God might overlook you or forget to care for your needs, "You established the earth, and it stands firm."

We could do this all day long. I could keep giving you verses from the Bible that would speak to your every fear, temptation, doubt, worry, anxiety, struggle, mistake, and regret.

But I think you get my point.

God has provided you with the deepest and richest resource you could ever imagine, filled with all the wisdom and instruction you will ever need in regard to all areas of life, particularly love and purity. He loves you too much to let you strike out on your own. He doesn't expect you to figure things out by yourself. His grace has provided you with the wisdom and instruction you need. If you will apply it and obey it, you cannot possibly miss His destiny for your life and for your marriage.

The first step toward your eternal destination of belonging to Jesus is the same as your first step toward true love, sexual purity, a great marriage, or an unmarried life devoted to Christ. It's simply submitting yourself and your desires to the loving instruction of God's Word.

Following His instructions points you in the right direction. Taking the right action gets you to the ultimate destination.

Jesus is the goal, the big win, the prize.

True Talk

1. Have you felt like, until this point in life, you've been heading in the right direction? Why or why not?

2. Have you decided what your ultimate destination is in life? If so, get a piece of paper, and write a sentence or two describing it.

3. If not, what further information do you need before making that decision? Spend time in God's Word and in prayer seeking that information.

4. On the same piece of paper where you've written your destination, list some "driving directions" that will help to get you there. Tuck your destination and your directions in your Bible or somewhere safe where you can refer to it any time that you need guidance.

CHAPTER 7

Hate It, Starve It, Outsmart It

I pray that He may grant you, according to the riches of His glory, to be strengthened with power in the inner man through His Spirit, and that the Messiah may dwell in your hearts through faith.

—Ephesians 3:16–17

Since I was old enough to comprehend conversations between adults, I have been fascinated with the history surrounding World War II. My grandfather was in the navy and fought for the Allies for four years in the South Pacific. He spoke about the war sparingly, but the stories he told us when I was a child captivated my young mind. I have long since made it a habit to read every good book and to record every interesting documentary I can find about World War II. I can't seem to get enough information about the greatest conflict in the history of humanity.

In 1941, the world seemed to be imploding. Europe was being overrun by Hitler's vast army. Jews were being systematically exterminated. Imperial Japan had been building a military force to rival our own and eventually attacked American forces in Hawaii at Pearl Harbor. The United States found itself neck-deep in a global conflict that was raging in Asia as well as Europe, and thoughts of winning against such strong enemies were small.

Turning the tide of the war would take more than soldiers and bullets. If the human race were to remain free, a concerted effort and a superior plan to defeat the Nazis and the Japanese was needed. Effort alone would never be sufficient. The Allies would have to launch a multifaceted attack if they hoped to have even the slightest chance at victory. (Stay with me here: this moment offers a priceless lesson.)

Great Britain, France, the United States, and our allies had to win in three different arenas: the ground, the air, and intelligence. Germany had a superior army and air force in Europe. Japan had a strong navy and air force in the Pacific. We would have to do more than match their strength. To defeat them, we would have to outwit them.

American factories began building tanks, guns, and artillery. Young men were drafted as GIs and trained to go to war. President Roosevelt conspired with British Prime Minister

Churchill. The smartest generals devised a plan that included every possible scenario and employed all possible weapons in an arsenal that would give the Allies the best chance at winning the war.

American forces stormed the beaches of Normandy, France, to establish a ground presence for the army to launch an offensive. Aircraft carriers transported fighters and bombers to Europe to push back the German attack on London and establish air superiority. Meanwhile, naval and ground forces converged in the South Pacific islands as Albert Einstein and others secretly worked on the first atomic bomb in a covert program called The Manhattan Project.

The plan did not depend on just one point of attack or a single offensive. The success of winning the war was predicated on all three elements: the ground, the air, and intelligence. We had to put troops on the ground. We had to get planes in the air. And we had to have better information. We would defeat our enemies if we could establish superiority in these three areas.

Our ground troops pushed across Europe, joining with British and French forces and pushing the Germans back into their own country. Our air force provided support and supplies to our forces in Europe and the Pacific. And our intelligence forces outwitted our enemies using spies and surveillance and ultimately by dropping two atomic bombs that ended a war that could have continued indefinitely and cost millions more lives. The world was saved from tyranny even though the enemy seemed much stronger.

Can we learn something from this old war story, maybe even specifically for our fight for holiness against temptation and sin? I believe we can.

You will never win the battle with sin (particularly sexual temptation) by just trying harder. Effort alone is not enough. Sin is stronger and more experienced than you. Sin is a serial killer, and like Hitler it will not settle for anything other than total dominion over your life. If you want to defeat sin and temptation, you have to have a better plan because you can't win with muscle. You'll have to do more than match its strength. You'll have to outwit sin with a better plan and employ a multifaceted attack.

Let's take a playbook from the Allies as they faced the Nazis and Imperial Japan. Instead of focusing on one aspect of your struggle, employ multiple weapons against the enemy. The Allies fought to dominate land, air, and intelligence. I want to suggest that you employ three tactics to gain victory over sexual sin and temptation.

Hate It. Starve It. Outsmart It.

The Power to Fight

The ability to launch an offensive against the creeping, rotting power of sin comes from the power of the Holy Spirit who dwells in you and makes your heart His home. If you think for even a second that you can outsmart sin, it will assassinate you before you can blink. Your ability to wage war against lust, insecurity, shame, and regret is rooted in the power of God that is at work within you right now. The apostle Paul speaks directly to us in this regard: "For this reason I kneel before the Father from whom every family in heaven and on earth is named. I pray that He may grant you, according to the riches of His glory, to be **strengthened with power** in the inner man **through His Spirit**, and that the Messiah may dwell in your hearts through faith" (Ephesians 3:14–17, emphasis added).

Our strength is not in a battle plan or a formula or human effort. Our strength is the Holy Spirit. We will win when we submit to the lordship of Christ and allow Him to dwell in our hearts through faith in His sacrifice, His promises, and His ability to keep us pure and holy. Any efforts that stand on our own strength, tactics, or tricks will only frustrate us as we grow more and more fatigued and eventually wallow in our own failure. The real battle is fought when we remember how powerless we are against an enemy as strong and seasoned as sin. If we can remember to rest in the strength of the Spirit who is at work in us, renewing us and transforming us, then the hardest part of the battle is essentially over: resting in His strength and submitting to His will.

So does this mean we don't need to do anything beyond remembering a few verses? Is anything required of you because Jesus has already made you holy and righteous through His sacrifice on the cross? And if the victory has already been won and sin has been defeated, why do the sin and the shame keep coming back at you again and again and again?

I have talked to thousands of students and adults (literally) who get so frustrated at their inability to stand up under the sexual temptations they face daily because in their hearts they believe they have victory in Christ, but in their daily lives they keep experiencing defeat. Many seem to be doing something wrong. They try to rely on the strength of the Holy Spirit. They read verses like the ones noted above in Ephesians 3. But they don't experience victory at all. They just keep giving in to the same sexual urges. Then they feel guilty and weak, and honestly many of them even begin to question their salvation. They doubt if they're Christians.

Here's an excerpt from a message a young woman sent me on Facebook. (She gave me permission to share with you.) I'm guessing a lot of you will relate.

> Dear Clayton,
>
> I know you are a busy guy, traveling and preaching all the time. But I really need your help because I feel like I am always trying so hard to get victory in the area of sexual purity, but I just keep failing over and over

again. I don't know whom to turn to. I listened to all of your messages on relationships, and you kept talking about finding our strength in Christ. You said Jesus had defeated sin in me when He died on the cross and was raised from the dead. I am a Christian and I have been saved for almost ten years, but I don't know HOW to win against sexual temptation. You said I had victory in Jesus, but if I really do, how does that work when I am being tempted to mess around with my boyfriend? I am not a virgin. I really love my boyfriend, and we're both Christians. We know it's wrong to sleep together, but we just can't stop. We pray, and we've even read the Bible together, but nothing works. I'd love to know HOW we can stop messing around because when you were preaching about it, it sounded so true and so easy. But then my boyfriend and I were together just hours after we both heard you preach, and we messed up again! I am so frustrated! I don't even know if I am a Christian anymore. I am doubting my own salvation. I am so confused. If I were really saved, I feel like this wouldn't be so hard. HELP!

Have you ever felt like her? I know I have. I also know it's not easy to break free from sex, lust, porn, or a bad relationship. But in Christ it is possible. Just as the Allies had to win the war on three fronts (air, land, intelligence), I think we wage war in three effective ways to win against the discouragement and frustration that always comes along with sexual sin.

The Battle Plan

The great British pastor and evangelist C. H. Spurgeon once said that even **though sinful thoughts may rise, they must not reign**. Your goal should be stopping sinful urges before they take control of you. Just because they rise in you, they don't have the right to reign over you. It is not a sin to be tempted because even Jesus was tempted to sin. You have to learn to stop temptation dead in its tracks before it turns into sin. I want to suggest a plan of attack that stands on the victory of Christ over sin while simultaneously moving forward based on your decision to fight against the ongoing power of temptation.

It's catchy and easy to remember. Say it with me.

Hate it. Starve it. Outsmart it.

1. Hate it. A decision must be made. You must take a position of absolute hatred toward sin. You decide you won't tolerate it. You get angry about the way it offends God. You despise the negative ways it hurts you and your body. You stop feeling sorry for yourself and take the offensive. No more whining and complaining! You categorize sexual sin along with things like the Ebola virus or bird flu; you despise it and avoid it! This is the only attitude that will work in the war on sin.

2. Starve it. Every enemy eventually loses if you cut off its food supply. The famous French general Napoleon Bonaparte once said that an army marches on its stomach. If you want to defeat sexual temptation, quit feeding it. This may mean breaking up with your boyfriend or girlfriend, putting filters on your computer, avoiding cable or high-speed Internet, or staying off Facebook. Stop going to parties where you know you'll meet people that just want to hook up. You have to get ruthless and starve your appetite for sexual sin. The longer you starve that appetite, the weaker it will get until it eventually starves to death.

3. Outsmart it. Get ahead of your enemy by predicting the ways you are tempted before you are tempted. Devise a plan that can't fail. Get crafty: decide that you'll never be alone with someone you want to mess around with. Ask a friend to hold you accountable daily in areas where you struggle. Choose to go only on group dates for a season of time. Don't have a TV or computer in your room. Turn off your smartphone every night at nine before you go into your room for bed. Read reviews of movies before you buy a ticket to make sure there's no sexual content. Don't be dumb. Outsmart the sin.

The basis for this approach is from the Old Testament. I've gone back to this passage of the Bible so many times I can quote it from memory. Check this out, and notice the words in bold.

> How I love Your instruction!
> It is my meditation all day long.
> Your commands make me **wiser** than my
>   enemies,
> for they are always with me.
> I have more **insight** than all my teachers
> because Your decrees are my meditation.
> I **understand** more than the elders
> because I obey your precepts.
> I have **kept my feet** from every evil path
> to follow Your word.
> I have not turned from Your judgments,
> for You Yourself have instructed me.
> How sweet Your word is to my taste—
> sweeter than honey in my mouth.
> I gain understanding from Your precepts;
> therefore I **hate** every false way.
> (Psalm 119:97–104, emphasis added)

The writer hates it. The last line plainly states that he hates every false way. I know *hate* is a strong word. And I know you were probably taught that you should never hate anyone. But this is not about hating a person. This is about hating what God hates, and God hates sin. Sin is one thing it's good to hate. You should hate every false way that leads you away from God and His plan for your life and your future.

Is it wrong to hate cancer? Is it a sin to hate rape? Is it bad to hate racism? No, no, and no. You know intuitively that it is good to hate bad things. Cancer, rape, and racism are terribly wicked things, and no one in their right minds would tolerate them. Sin is more devastating than all of these; it is eternally destructive. Hating sin is the first step toward defeating it. God hates sin. You belong to God. You must hate sin too.

The writer starves it. He says he's kept his feet from every evil path to follow God's Word. He decided he would not feed any evil desire. He would not walk in the path that led to wicked places. He would avoid things and people that led to sinful outcomes. Instead of moving toward sin and temptation, he moved away from them by going a different direction. He pursued something better: the Word of God.

In the same way you too can starve your appetite for sexual or romantic sin. It's not enough to cut off the food supply because you will still be hungry. Instead of feasting on sin, you feast on God. You read His Word, meditate on His wisdom, build your relationship with Christ through prayer and worship and service. Your faith will grow stronger as you feed it. Lust and temptation will grow weaker as you starve them and keep your feet from every evil path.

The writer outsmarts it. Look again at the passage above. The writer says that God's commands make him "wiser" than his enemies, that he has more "insight" than his teachers, and that he "understands" more than the elders because he obeys God's precepts. It's pretty clear that submitting to God's Word is the only way you can outsmart sin. You already know you can't win by yourself. You've probably tried that and failed. The good news, however, is that you don't have to devise some complex plan full of intricate details and tricks to gain victory over temptation. The way you outsmart sexual sin is to read the Bible, know the Bible, and obey the Bible. It all comes back to the big idea behind the *True Love Project*: Jesus is Lord, and He calls the shots. If we trust Him, we will do what He says. And if you want to know what He says, you find it in His Word.

Outsmart sin by applying the ancient wisdom of Scripture. It's tried, tested, and true. The smartest thing you can ever do is to follow the smartest One you've ever known, and that would be God.

Adopt and Adapt

You will need to *adopt* this battle plan and *adapt* it to your situation. Although each of us struggles with sexual temptation, those desires will look different in each individual life, ranging from same-sex attraction to a strong appetite for porn. Your issue may be vivid memories of sexual abuse you can't get rid of, or it may be the overpowering pull on your heart to go back to an ex-boyfriend or ex-girlfriend anytime you feel lonely or depressed.

Adapt your strategy according to your enemy. Get creative and flexible with this. Your enemy is sin. Jesus has given you victory over sin. You are learning to live out that victory by waging war against temptation daily. You are learning to rely on the power of the Holy Spirit to resist those temptations by getting aggressive and taking the offensive against sexual sin by hating it, starving it, and outsmarting it.

One of my best friends is a pastor in Charlotte, North Carolina. While writing a book together several years ago, we came up with the "hate it, starve it, outsmart it" idea. He had a strange but effective way of adapting this approach to his own situation.

He and his wife had only been married a short time. Because she had shopped at Victoria's Secret, their address was added to the database of customers, and they began receiving Victoria's Secret catalogs at their home. Now if you know anything about Victoria's Secret, you know there really aren't any secrets. It's pretty much all out in the open. The pictures in the sales catalogs may seem harmless to many women, but for most of the guys I've talked to, a Victoria's Secret catalog is one step short of soft-core porn. The images on those pages become locked into a man's mind once he views shapely female supermodels in their underwear. It can also lead to a curiosity and appetite for more images with even less clothing. Just as marijuana becomes a doorway drug for other addictions, these magazines become a doorway for young men (and even some young women) to more graphic images.

He decided to cut off the temptation before it arrived. He called Victoria's Secret and asked to be removed from their mailing list, but the catalogs kept coming. He called again, but they kept appearing in his mailbox. He would throw them away, but he would always remember they were in the trash can, and he was strangely drawn back to them, imagining retrieving them from the garbage to look at the women modeling seductive undergarments.

He adjusted his game plan and began adapting his strategy. When a catalog came in the mail, he took it inside, took it to his bathroom, lifted the toilet seat, plunged the magazine into the toilet, and swirled it around several times. Then he put the waterlogged magazine in the trash can. He wanted to make sure he cut off all possibility of being drawn back to a temptation he'd already resisted. The dirty toilet water was an added incentive to keep him from digging it out of the garbage.

He was hating it, starving it, and outsmarting it. He got serious about holiness. He cut off the food supply by starving his mind of the potential to look at those pictures. He adapted his battle plan to the nature of the temptation, and it worked.

This is how you should approach all the battles you will face in your fight for purity. Make no mistake: it *is* a war! And if you're going to win, you will need to adjust your approach to

> For our battle is not against flesh and blood, but against the rulers, against the authorities, against the world powers of this darkness, against the spiritual forces of evil in the heavens.
> —Ephesians 6:12

the situations you face. Whether you use toilet water or a trash can or both, use this template as your starting place: Hate it. Starve it. Outsmart it.

Other Battle Plans

• I have a friend who calls me whenever he is traveling to let me know he is in a hotel by himself. He asks me to hold him accountable in what he watches. He asks me to pray for him that he will not look at anything online or on TV that will cause him regret or guilt. Then he promises me out loud that he will guard his eyes and his heart and not view any-thing that would dishonor God.

• Three men I know have signed up for an online filtering service. Each of them has a history with porn addiction, and this service not only blocks them from visiting bad websites, but it also records every website they access on their comput-ers and devices and sends me an e-mail once a week so I can see every site they've visited.

• A college student struggled with same-sex attraction, particularly homosexual pornography. He said it was the result of being molested by his uncle when he was a young boy. When he became a Christian, he and his roommates sat down one night and deleted his Facebook account and all of the contacts in his phone that would be a temptation for him. He knew the allure of his old lifestyle, and he was determined to outsmart the sin.

• Four high school girls made a covenant to God and to one another that they would not get involved in a serious relationship with a boy until they had memorized the book of Philippians and had been on two international mission trips with their church. They said they wanted to be grounded in the Word and actively carrying out the Great Commission before they started thinking about boys and love and dating. They wanted to be spiritually mature before they pursued a relationship.

• An old friend who is an evangelist like me has a ritual he goes through every time he enters a hotel room on a trip to preach. He unplugs the TV, turns it around backward, covers it with a towel, and places pictures of his wife and kids on top of the TV or in front of it. That's ruthless! He makes it hard to sin and unlikely that he will give in to temptation.

• A student at a church where I frequently preach has chosen never to be alone with a guy after ten o'clock at night. She also committed to her parents that she would only date a guy who loved Jesus, was actively involved in serving at his church, and was willing to come to her house and meet her mom and dad and siblings. She also said she wanted any guy she dated to spend a day getting to know her dad before she would go out on a date alone with him. *That* is a battle plan!

You could call each of these an example of good, old-fashioned self-control. The human effort required for self-control is rooted in the power of the Holy Spirit. Because He lives in us, we have the power to change our attitudes and habits and desires. Hating it, starving it, and outsmarting it takes effort, but the apostle Peter tells us that effort pays off:

> For this very reason, **make every effort** to supplement your faith with goodness, goodness with knowledge, knowledge with **self-control**, self-control with endurance, endurance with godliness, godliness with brotherly affection, and brotherly affection with love. For if these

qualities are yours and are increasing, they will keep you from being useless or unfruitful in the knowledge of our Lord Jesus Christ. (2 Peter 1:5–8, emphasis added)

Fighting from Victory, Not for Victory

Every Christian needs to understand one simple truth in our battle for holiness. When it comes to sexual sin, the battle has already been fought, and the victory has already been won. **You are not fighting FOR victory. You are fighting FROM victory.**

When Jesus was raised from the dead, He proved once and for all that all power and authority in the universe and beyond belong to Him. No one had ever defeated the enemy of death before, but Jesus did. And He gave us a glimpse into the power of His kingdom.

Because Jesus Christ lives in you through the Holy Spirit, you have the power to resist temptation. He has made you holy, and *holiness is both a position and a pursuit.* Because you are a child of God by faith, your *position* in His family is secure. Because He has filled you with His Holy Spirit, you have the power to *pursue* purity and resist temptation from your position as a forgiven, redeemed child of the King. And when you give up lordship of your life to the One true Lord, you gain the power to live a holy life. The fight against sexual sin is won by faith—trusting that Jesus has something better for you than the momentary pleasure of giving into your urges and desires.

When Jesus died on the cross, the Gospels record the last words He uttered before He died: "It is finished." This did not mean *He* was finished. It meant the mission He came to accomplish had been completed. He had lived a holy and perfect life for all of us who could never be holy and perfect on our own. He had suffered and died in our place when we deserved to be punished for our sins. He had destroyed the work of the devil and the power of sin, not with a sword or a spear or thunder and lightning but through humility and submission to His Father. And in the face of temptation, even face-to-face with Satan himself, Jesus never wavered to the left or the right. He remained faithful to His mission.

When He proclaimed, "It is finished," He declared *our* victory over sin, death, hell, and judgment. He was announcing the kingdom of God in all its power and beauty. God had won, and Satan had lost. The curse would be reversed, and new life was now available to all who would believe in Him. His power gives you victory over guilt, shame, insecurity, regret, and temptation. The ultimate battle was fought two thousand years ago. The ultimate victory has already been won. The winner has been declared, and it is Jesus. Because you belong to Jesus, you are one with Him; you are just as victorious as He is. His victory is your victory. **You are holy** in your position as His possession, and you are empowered to pursue holiness, making every effort to demonstrate self-control.

So you are not in this battle alone. And the victory is already yours. You must learn how to act like the victor. You need to learn how to live in the victory Jesus won for you. You are not fighting *for* victory. You are fighting *from* victory.

You Can Be Free

The United States hasn't gone to war with the British during our lifetime. Why would we? They are our closest allies! But things weren't always this way. Nearly 250 years ago our ancestors were living under the tyranny of the British Empire. They declared their independence from England and launched the Revolutionary War. The Americans won, and we became a free people. You and I have never once fired a shot at a British soldier, but we enjoy the freedoms our ancestors won for us every single day because they fought a war that was for us. They won the victory for us. We have freedom because of their sacrifice.

In the same way Christ is the Victor, and you and I are the recipients of the bounty of His victory. Paul celebrates this—and we can too—in the words below:

> When this corruptible is clothed with incor-
> ruptibility, and this mortal is clothed with

immortality, then the saying that is written will take place: **Death has been swallowed up in victory. Death, where is your victory? Death, where is your sting?** Now the sting of death is sin, and the power of sin is the law. But thanks be to God, who gives us the victory through our Lord Jesus Christ! Therefore, my dear brothers, be steadfast, immovable, always excelling in the Lord's work, knowing that your labor in the Lord is not in vain. (1 Corinthians 15:54–58, emphasis added)

Just as our ancestors fought for our freedom long before we were born, Jesus bled and died for your freedom thousands of years ago. He faced an opponent you could have never defeated, but through His sacrifice on the cross, He triumphed over the enemy. He allows us to enjoy the benefits of His victory.

Because He was faithful, you can be free.

True Talk

1. What are some specific things you are battling? Racy photos on your phone? A certain guy? Secret thoughts?

2. For each of those things you're struggling with, create a three-part battle plan (hate it, starve it, outsmart it) for each item. (Look back at the examples in the chapter if you need ideas.)

3. Find a trusted friend or mentor who can help hold you accountable. Share your battle plan with him or her, and ask for prayer as you learn to claim victory as your own.

4. Do you have friends facing some of the same struggles? Share with them your plan of attack and help them talk through creating their own.

CHAPTER 8

Sex, God's Glory, and Your Mission

But honor the Messiah as Lord in your hearts. Always be ready to give a defense to anyone who asks you for a reason for the hope that is in you.

—1 Peter 3:15

Since the beginning of the church, the Christian perspective on sexuality has always made us stand out like a city on a hill. It's been one of the defining characteristics of the movement that Jesus began. Intrinsic to the gospel is a belief that we don't think and act like the world when it comes to marriage and how we treat human bodies (our own and those we are in relationship with). In his masterful book *The Rise of Christianity* Rodney Stark makes it clear from history that one of the major reasons the Christian faith found traction and took root in the ancient world as well as the Middle Ages was precisely because of how Christians viewed sexuality.

When followers of Jesus declared that they would not be caught up in the tide of culturally accepted norms that violated Christian conviction, it was a powerful, undeniable witness to the world. Men treated their wives as partners, not servants. Men refused to have multiple wives. Husbands and wives practiced purity, before and after marriage. Although ancient Greek, Roman, and European cultures participated in every kind of debauchery, Christians maintained their witness by living and loving differently than the cultures they lived in. Marriage was a holy and sacred covenant that reflected the relationship between Jesus and His bride, the church. Now 2,000 years after Jesus walked on this Earth, this is still one of the most powerful witnesses to the truth of the gospel that an unbelieving world will ever see.

Every Christian is a missionary.

When you become a follower of Christ, you are doing more than joining a club with eternal benefits like heaven and streets of gold. You are also joining a movement that has changed our entire world and the course of history itself.

You are signing up for a rescue mission.

You are becoming a member of God's family, and that family is called the church. The church is more than an organization; it is a living, breathing, missionary movement that exists to glorify God by making disciples of all people from all nations.

As a child of God, you were rescued from sin. And now God wants to use you in His plan to rescue others from sin so they can experience the same relationship with Jesus you have.

God didn't save you so you could sit. He saved you so you could serve.

He didn't save you to wait around. He saved you to work and worship.

Our Worship Is Our Witness to the World

As you think about your faith in Jesus, remember that everything revolves around lordship. We must continually ask ourselves, "Who is lord?" The answer to that question will clarify what you should do and how you should act and how you should treat others at any given moment. It's the most important question you'll ever ask as a Christian because it always brings you back to Jesus.

As we've learned, when Jesus is Lord of your life, He is Lord of *all* of your life, including your physical and emotional desires for romance, love, and sex. I want you to consider how your commitment to living a holy life, set apart for Christ, is actually an act of worship as well as a witness to the world.

When we realize that our bodies belong to the Lord and that the Holy Spirit lives in us, it is a massive revelation! It causes us to rethink how we live, what we watch, how we act, and even how we think. We consecrate ourselves in light of the presence of God.

If you found out that the president of the United States was coming to eat dinner at your house this week, you'd be helping your mom prepare by cleaning the house, vacuuming the floors, dusting the shelves, and scouring the bathrooms. You would do that to honor the president and to create a clean and inviting environment. The same concept applies to your body and soul. **Because Jesus lives in you, you realize the importance of creating an environment in your mind and heart where He is honored and placed above all other things.**

This is an act of worship. To worship Christ means you place Him above all other things in this world. You give Him the highest place. He has the ultimate position of prominence and honor in your life. Worship becomes more than singing songs at church or youth camp. It becomes a lifestyle where you constantly place your mind's attention and your heart's affection on Jesus Christ. You begin to decrease, and He begins to increase (John 3:30). He becomes bigger and you become smaller. Your life becomes focused more on Him and less on you. This is the essence of worship.

Perhaps the most important area in the life of young men and women where we must set apart Christ as the object of our worship is the area of sex and relationships. You may have never thought about it this way, but when you pursue holiness here, it is actually an act of worship.

You are declaring to God that you choose His desires over your own selfish cravings. You are denying your flesh and allowing the Holy Spirit to guide you. You are giving Jesus the highest place in the area where you probably struggle the most. You are saying to God, "I take Your Word seriously; and with the help of Your Spirit, I'm going to turn my sexual desires over to Your wisdom, put my relationships in Your hands, and follow Your ways." This is tough to do, for sure. But it's the right thing to do, and it ultimately brings glory to God and joy to you.

It is a complete and total act of worship to stand against the tide of sexual sin and temptation and to declare, "Jesus is Lord and I belong to Him. I will do what He says."

And when you worship the Lord by surrendering this area to Him, He uses that as your witness to the world.

Stand Up and Speak Out

I learned how my commitment to sexual purity became a witness to those around me when I was a sophomore in high school.

I attended a Christian school until my freshman year, but I transferred to public school as a sophomore. I wanted to pursue football, and I wanted to begin a ministry on a public school campus. So I made the varsity football team, and I met with the principal the first day of classes to find out what I needed to do to start a Christian club on campus. I was on a mission. I really sensed the Lord leading me there, and I wanted to use football as a platform to reach my friends with the gospel.

Little did I know that not only would God use my place on the football team as a witness to my school, but He would also use my commitment to sexual purity.

On the first day of Honors English, our teacher handed out the syllabus and our first book we would read as a class. It was *The Scarlet Letter.* You may have read it yourself. But if not, it's an American literary classic set in Puritan New England. The teacher gave us a brief overview of what it was about: a woman in the 1600s who gets pregnant in a Puritan village. She is ridiculed and judged and treated with contempt. She refuses to give the name of the baby's father and becomes an outcast who is forced to wear a giant red letter *A* on her clothes, identifying her as guilty of adultery.

When the teacher finished setting the stage for the book, the class erupted into a discussion about sex. Granted, these were smart students in the Honors program, and they all knew one another. I was the new guy, and I didn't know anyone. The conversation was lively! It quickly turned from a discussion about the literary style of the book into personal confessions of sexual activity.

I couldn't believe what I was hearing. Sophomores in high school were publicly declaring how many people they had had sex with. One guy said: "I hate it when religious people try to tell me what I can and can't do. They are such hypocrites!" Then a girl in the class exclaimed, "Yeah, what's the big deal about sex anyway? Why do people get so worked up over it? I've had sex with lots of guys."

The whole class was laughing and obviously agreeing with them: sex is no big deal, and no one can tell us what to do.

As the conversation continued, I felt my heart rate skyrocket. My head got hot, and my palms got sweaty. I knew I had to speak up. I wanted to be a voice for the gospel in that moment. But I knew that if I did, I would be branded as a religious nut or a fanatic.

I was the new guy. This was the first day of class. If I shared my convictions, there was no turning back.

I gathered my courage and spoke: "I know I'm the new guy here, but I can't believe what I am hearing. Most of us are fifteen or sixteen years old in here. Do you all really believe that sleeping around with whomever you're dating at the time is a healthy way to live? That just cheapens sex, makes it meaningless. Don't you ever feel bad after you break up?"

As soon as I said that, they began to fire back at me. They called me a Bible beater and a holy roller. They laughed at the fact that I would even question their view on sex as a recreational sport on a date. But the real moment of truth came when one student looked at me and asked the question I could not avoid.

"What are you, some kind of virgin?"

And at that moment I understood what it meant to be a witness for the gospel. There was no way I could dodge the question. I had to answer it. I could either tell the truth, or I could tell a lie, but the spotlight was now on me.

For a split second I considered giving a vague response. I wanted to fit in. I wanted to be popular and sit with these kids at lunch. They were the cool kids. They were the smart kids. And how I answered that question would dictate where I fit every single day at school for the next three years.

But in that moment I also sensed the Holy Spirit giving me courage. I knew He wanted me to use my convictions about sexual purity as a platform to be a witness for Jesus Christ. I clearly remember what I said.

"Yes, I am a virgin. And I hope to be a virgin when I get married. I believe that sex is so powerful and beautiful that it should be saved for marriage. I believe that because I am a Christian, and I've committed my life to Jesus. I live according to His Word."

For a split second there was total silence. Everyone—including my teacher—stared at me in confusion and disbelief. I felt like an exotic animal at the zoo.

Then all of a sudden, the whole class erupted in laughter. They made fun of me. They mocked me for being a virgin. One girl even said that I was stupid for waiting to have sex on my honeymoon night—that if I remained a virgin, I wouldn't know what to do with a naked woman once I got her in bed.

It was harsh, to say the least. I felt their disdain, but I also felt the courage of my faith in Jesus as He gave me the words to say in that moment. I knew they would pick on me for the next three years. **I knew I would never fit into their clique. But that was OK because that wasn't my mission.** I didn't go to public school to fit in with the crowd. I went there to stand out, to be a witness that Jesus had changed my life and to let them know that He could change their lives too.

I look back on that day in tenth grade as one of the most significant moments of my life. I knew it would be hard to say no to sex, but I had no idea how hard it would be to stand up to the peer pressure of everyone else's expectations. Honestly, it was more difficult at first to be seen as the weirdo who was a virgin. But eventually some of those same students who ridiculed me for my faith came to ask me for advice and prayer. Because I was willing to be a witness, I was also the friend they could turn to when their relationships fell apart and they were discouraged and confused.

Don't be afraid to be bold about Jesus. Don't be afraid of what people may say and think. It doesn't matter if you fit in with the crowd because the crowd always changes directions and can never be trusted. Jesus never changes, and you can always trust in Him. You belong to Him. And when you are vocal about your commitment to Christ and His design for love and sexual purity, you will stand out as one who belongs to Him.

Spared and Prepared

Remember, God doesn't hand down arbitrary, random rules just to watch us squirm. Obeying Him always has an eternal benefit. It's not always easy at first. Often our obedience leads to short-term suffering, hardship, or pain. But ultimately obedience to God is for our own good because it leads us to something better.

I forbade my son from overdosing on Krispy Kreme doughnuts because I knew what was best for him. I wanted to spare my son from a sugar crash and sick stomach in the short term and rotten teeth and obesity in the long term. A good daddy wants to spare his children from things that hurt them, and God is a good Father. He warns us to avoid sexual sin so we can be spared from all the harmful effects and consequences that will follow us for the rest of our lives.

We've seen how secular experts, modern scientists, and medical doctors have all affirmed what God knew all along: sex with anyone outside of a loving, committed marriage is harmful. When a doctor warns you to change your behavior or to avoid something that will hurt you, it's for your own good. How much more should you listen to God and be spared the pain and regret of stubborn disobedience?

Saying no to a small thing seems hard at the time, but if it leads to something much bigger and better, it makes perfect sense. Every time you submit your body, your imagination, or your relationships to Jesus, you are growing and maturing into the kind of woman or man that will one day be ready for a fulfilling and wonderful marriage (and yes, the sex can be amazing too).

The great NBA player Larry Bird had a reputation for being one of the best shooters in the league. He drained three-pointers throughout his career and made some amazing shots in clutch situations. To the average fan watching on TV, it looked as if he were just naturally gifted as a shooter.

But that wasn't true.

He would arrive early to practice and shoot hundreds of three-pointers. He would stay after practice and shoot for another hour after his teammates had gone home. He took thousands of practice shots. That's why he made the game shots. He prepared.

Practice makes you prepared. The more you practice purity, the more prepared you are for marriage. The more you practice self-control, the more prepared you will be to stay dedicated to your spouse. The more you practice sacrifice, the more prepared you are to be a witness to the world that the gospel does, in fact, work.

It takes faith to sacrifice your desires to Jesus. But in the end you don't lose anything at all. You gain the blessing of being prepared for what you wanted all along.

True Talk

1. What are some ways you've been a missionary for Christ?

2. Have you ever been a part of a scene like that in my sophomore English class? What happened? What did you do?

3. What is one way you can begin today to share God's glory through your story?

4. So, do you feel prepared for your mission? Take a moment to put your mission into words. Then write a Bible verse (or ten!) underneath that gives you strength and courage for that mission.

Still Fighting.
Still on a Mission.

When I finished writing the *True Love Project*, I was forty years old and celebrating fourteen years of marriage with Sharie. We have two awesome boys and a great life in ministry together. She helped me write this project, and we are the best of friends.

But I am still fighting for purity. At forty years old, I still battle lust. I still have to turn away from certain billboards. I still turn my head in the airport or on the beach. I have to guard my eyes when I'm watching TV or when I'm online. The battle for holiness never stops, no matter how old you get.

And did you know that my testimony of fighting for sexual purity is still a witness to the world?

Right as I was wrapping up the *True Love Project*, I happened to be preaching in Greensboro, North Carolina. One morning I was getting coffee at the hotel restaurant where I was staying, and my assistant was with me. Jordan is twenty-five years old, and the guy behind the counter was kidding around with me. He asked me if Jordan was my son.

I responded, "No way! That would mean that I had a son when I was fifteen years old!"

The man behind the counter said, "Well that's pretty normal these days. Kids start having sex when they're twelve or thirteen."

I remembered how God had used my testimony in tenth grade. I remembered how scared I was to speak up but how God eventually allowed me to influence some of those students who ridiculed me. And twenty-five years later He was still giving me that opportunity.

I answered the guy, "Not everyone starts having sex at twelve or thirteen. I didn't. I was a virgin when I got married, and I've only had sex with one woman in my whole life."

"You've got to be kidding me!" he shouted for the whole restaurant to hear. "No way. How did you do it? *Why* did you do it?"

I am telling you with absolute certainty that when you let Jesus be Lord of your relationships and submit your sexuality to Him, people will take notice. They will ask questions. They will be intrigued. And that will be your witness to the world.

So I told him. I explained how I'd become a Christian at fourteen, how I had given my life to Jesus, including my physical body. I told him I'd made mistakes, but when I did, I repented and received God's forgiveness. I told Him God gave me the strength to wait until I was married—and that when I did, I married a twenty-four-year-old virgin. But most importantly, I told him that it was all because of Jesus Christ.

The man smiled and said, "Wow, that's crazy. I can't believe that. But I respect you for it. I wish more people did that."

I'm not promising you that people will celebrate your commitment to purity or applaud your battle for holiness. Many won't. It will not be easy.

But you're on a mission.

You represent the kingdom of God, and you carry the gospel of Jesus Christ with you everywhere you go. And every day you're coming face-to-face with people who are lost, confused, and far from God. There is no better way for you to share the love and joy Jesus brings than to live counterculturally, by going against the flow and pursuing holiness as an act of worship to God. People will be drawn to your story, and God can use your story to change theirs.

Believe me, I've been there. And I know.

This is the only lasting way to find true love.

Notes

Chapter 1: God's Story, Your Story

1. Timothy Keller, *The Meaning of Marriage* (New York: Dutton Press, 2011), 227.

Chapter 2: The Cost of Ownership

1. G. K. Chesterton, *Orthodoxy* (New York: John Lane Company, 1909), 269.

2. Timothy Keller, *The Meaning of Marriage* (New York: Dutton Press, 2011).

Chapter 3: The Bible on Sex

1. Timothy Keller, *The Meaning of Marriage* (New York: Dutton Press, 2011).

2. Joe S. McIlhaney Jr. and Freda McKissic Bush, *Hooked: New Science on How Casual Sex Is Affecting Our Children* (Chicago: Northfield Publishing, 2008).

3. R. P. Lederman, W. Chan, and C. Roberts-Gray, "Sexual Risk Attitudes and Intentions of Youth Aged 12–14 Years: Survey Comparisons of Parent-Teen Prevention and Control Groups," *Behavioral Medicine* 29, no. 4 (2004): 155–63.

4. M. D. Resnick, P. S. Bearman, R. W. Blum, et al., "Protecting Adolescents from Harm; Findings from the National Longitudinal Study on Adolescent Health," *JAMA* 278, no. 10 (1997): 823–32.

5. C. McNeely, M. L. Shew, T. Beuring, et al., "Mothers' Influence on the Timing of First Sex among 14- and 15-Year-Olds," *Journal of Adolescent Health* 31, no. 3 (2002); 251–73.

Chapter 4: Your Heart Matters

1. Joe S.,McIlhaney Jr. and Freda McKissic Bush, *Hooked: New Science on How Casual Sex Is Affecting Our Children* (Chicago: Northfield Publishing, 2008), 101.
2. Ibid., 137.
3. Ibid., 100.
4. Ibid., 77.
5. J. Elman, E. A. Bates, M. Johnson, et al., *Rethinking Innateness: A Connectionist Perspective on Development* (Cambridge, MA: MIT Press, 1997).
6. O. Arias-Carrion, E. Poppel, "Dopamine, Learning and Reward-Seeking Behavior," *Acta Neurobiologiae Expermintalis* 67, no. 4 (2007): 481–88.
7. McIlhaney and Bush, *Hooked*, 39.
8. J. R. Kahn, K. A. London, "Premarital Sex and the Risk of Divorce," *Journal of Marriage and the Family* 53 (November 1991): 845–55.
9. Ibid.
10. R. Finger, et al., "Association of Virginity at Age 18 with Educational Economic, Social and Health Outcomes in Middle Adulthood," *Adolescent and Family Health* 3, no. 4 (2004): 164–70.
11. McIlhaney and Bush, *Hooked*, 82–83.
12. Centers for Disease Control and Prevention. Youth Risk Behavior Surveillance: United States, 2005. Surveillance Summaries, 2006. MMWR 2006, 55.

Chapter 5: Purity from Within

1. Wilfred A. Peterson, *The Art of Living Treasure Chest* (New York: Simon and Schuster, 1977).
2. Lewis B. Smedes, *The Art of Forgiving* (New York: Ballantine Books, 1997), 63.
3. Ibid.
4. Ibid., 21.
5. Ibid., 73.
6. Ibid., 66.
7. Ibid., 29.

Chapter 6: Direction and Destination

1. Wendy Farley, *The Wounding and Healing of Desire: Weaving Heaven and Earth* (Louisville: Westminster John Knox, 2005).

About the Authors

Clayton King is president of Clayton King Ministries and Crossroads Summer Camps, the teaching pastor at Newspring Church, and campus pastor at Liberty University. He is an evangelist, author, and missionary. Clayton began preaching at the age of fourteen and has traveled to thirty-six countries and forty-six states. He's written nine books and preached to more than three million people. Clayton is passionate about seeing people far from God repent of their sin and begin a relationship with Jesus. He loves to pastor pastors and empower Christians for ministry. He also loves four-wheelers, action figures, black coffee, and his wife and two sons.

Sharie King was saved at the age of eleven and sensed God calling her to share her story of rescue and redemption. She has shared the gospel at Crossroads camps, college campuses, and mission trips in countries like Poland, India, and Malaysia. She is the vision developer and speaker for Clayton King Ministries as well as the founder of Ladies Only, the women's ministry division. Sharie speaks at women's events in local churches and conferences across America, teaching